OLYMPIAD WORKBOOK

INTERNATIONAL MATHEMATICS OLYMPIAD

- **01** Learning Objectives
- **02** Multiple Choice Questions
- **03** HOTS (Achievers Section)
- **04** Model Test Paper
- **05** Answer Keys and Solutions
- **06** OMR Answer Sheet

V&S PUBLISHERS

Published by:

V&S PUBLISHERS

F-2/16, Ansari road, Daryaganj, New Delhi-110002
☎ 23240026, 23240027 • *Fax:* 011-23240028
✉ info@vspublishers.com • ⊕ www.vspublishers.com

 **Online Brandstore: amazon.in/vspublishers**

Regional Office : Hyderabad
5-1-707/1, Brij Bhawan (Beside Central Bank of India Lane)
Bank Street, Koti, Hyderabad - 500 095
☎ 040-24737290
✉ vspublishershyd@gmail.com

Follow us on:   

BUY OUR BOOKS FROM: | AMAZON | | FLIPKART |

© **Copyright:** V&S PUBLISHERS
ISBN 978-81-977325-6-0
New Edition

DISCLAIMER

While every attempt has been made to provide accurate and timely information in this book, neither the author nor the publisher assumes any responsibility for errors, unintended omissions or commissions detected therein. The author and publisher makes no representation or warranty with respect to the comprehensiveness or completeness of the contents provided.

All matters included have been simplified under professional guidance for general information only, without any warranty for applicability on an individual. Any mention of an organization or a website in the book, by way of citation or as a source of additional information, doesn't imply the endorsement of the content either by the author or the publisher. It is possible that websites cited may have changed or removed between the time of editing and publishing the book.

Results from using the expert opinion in this book will be totally dependent on individual circumstances and factors beyond the control of the author and the publisher.

It makes sense to elicit advice from well informed sources before implementing the ideas given in the book. The reader assumes full responsibility for the consequences arising out from reading this book.

For proper guidance, it is advisable to read the book under the watchful eyes of parents/guardian. The buyer of this book assumes all responsibility for the use of given materials and information.

The copyright of the entire content of this book rests with the author/publisher. Any infringement/transmission of the cover design, text or illustrations, in any form, by any means, by any entity will invite legal action and be responsible for consequences thereon.

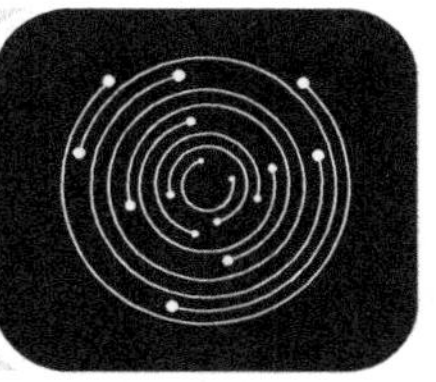

V&S Publishers has carved a significant niche in the publishing industry over the last decade, having successfully published more than 1000 titles across 9 languages spanning over 50 subject categories. Being known for the quality of content, we have built a reputation of excellence and reliability. We have consistently delivered **"Value & Substance"** to our readers, through a wide range of titles across a variety of genres covering school books, fiction and non-fiction that caters to different people from every section of the society.

The **Olympiad Guidebooks for classes 1-10** across all subjects, launched almost a decade ago, under the **GEN X Imprint**, became a go-to-source for the school students in no time, owing to their invaluable and substantive content written in a guidebook pattern,.

Having successfully sold a million copies of the same and in response to demand by both students as well as shopkeepers nationwide; we now present before you our newly launched **Olympiad Workbook Series**, designed for **classes 1-10 across 4 subjects**.

The workbooks are meticulously curated by a team of experienced educators, researchers and subject matter experts, edited by professionals and peer reviewed by teachers. The team has poured its efforts and expertise into creating a crisp and concise workbook which will help and guide the students to the path of success in Olympiad exams. The **MCQs** identified will not only help in scoring top marks in Olympiads but also inculcate a sense of deeper understanding of the subject, by way of solving **HOTS** and referring to complete solutions at the end of the book.

Here we present our new release– **OLYMPIAD WORKBOOK (IMO) CLASS–5** having following features:

- ☞ Based on the latest syllabi
- ☞ MCQs with comprehensive coverage of topics
- ☞ HOTS Questions liberally included
- ☞ A dedicated chapter on logical reasoning
- ☞ Model test paper for thorough practice
- ☞ Sample OMR sheet for real time simulation

We have made sure through our best efforts, that this workbook strictly follows the latest syllabi and patterns of the Olympiad Examination.

As **V&S Publishers** continuously strive to enhance the readability and maintain the credibility of our academic publications, we seek the support of our valuable readers in influencing and enriching the lives of future generations of students.

P.S. While every care has been taken to ensure the correctness of the content, if you come across any error, howsoever minor, do not hesitate to discuss with teachers while pointing that out to us in no uncertain terms.

We wish you all the best for your exams!

DISTINCTIVE FEATURES

01 Learning Objectives

They list the whole chapter as subtopics, helping the teachers to guide children in a step-by-step manner.

02 Multiple Choice Questions

MCQs act as an excellent learning aid, helping you to understand and work on your mistakes.

03 HOTS (Achievers Section)

The High Order Thinking Questions aim to help the student to solve Application-based questions and gain practical understanding of the subject.

04 Model Test Paper

Model test paper are provided at the end of each book, which help the student to test the knowledge which they have gained after thorough reading of all chapters.

05 Answer Key

Detailed Answer Key along with explanations aid the pupil to indentify, understand the mistakes they make during the course of Olympiad preparation.

CONTENTS

NUMBER SYSTEM

LEARNING OBJECTIVES

- ➤ Number System
- ➤ Numerals
- ➤ Fractions
- ➤ Imaginary Numbers
- ➤ Types of Numbers
- ➤ Place Value
- ➤ Number Sense
- ➤ Number Names
- ➤ Integers

MULTIPLE CHOICE QUESTIONS

1. What is the predecessor of the greatest six-digit number?
  (A) 100000 (B) 100001
  (C) 999998 (D) 999999

2. What is the difference between the place values of 5's in the number 4598351?
  (A) 499950 (B) 49995
  (C) 49950 (D) 0

3. 9,87,61,230 ☐ 9,87,16,230
  Which of the following signs can be placed in the box between the two numbers?
  (A) > (B) <
  (C) = (D) None of these

4. 10000001 is the successor of _______
  (A) 10000002 (B) 10000000
  (C) 9999999 (D) None of these

5. How many three-digit numbers can be formed with the digits 3, 0 and 7 without repetition?
  (A) 6 (B) 5
  (C) 4 (D) 3

6. Which are the respective greatest and the smallest numbers amongst 321987, 319240, 321978 and 321970?
  (A) 319240 and 321987
  (B) 321987 and 319240
  (C) 321987 and 321970
  (D) 319240 and 321978

7. What is the difference between the greatest and smallest 5-digit numbers formed by using all the digits 3, 0, 9, 1 and 5?
  (A) 93951 (B) 84951
  (C) 81720 (D) 79172

8. Which of the following numbers is equal to 3 crore?
  (A) 3 million (B) 30 million
  (C) 300 million (D) 3000 million

9. How can the number fifty million twenty-one thousand two hundred thirty six be written using commas according to Indian system of numeration?
  (A) 50,021,236 (B) 5,00,21,236
  (C) 50,00,21,236 (D) 500,021,236

10. How can the numbers 10 million, 1 billion and 216 thousand be arranged in descending order?

(A) 216 thousand, 10 million, 1 billion

(B) 10 million, 216 thousand, 1 billion

(C) 1 billion, 10 million, 216 thousand

(D) 216 thousand, 1 billion, 10 million

11. 2,357,822 ☐ 2,357,799

(A) <

(B) >

(C) =

(D) None of these

12. The number 35 million ends with how many zeroes?

(A) Four

(B) Five

(C) Six

(D) Seven

13. Which one of the following numbers is prime?

(A) 18

(B) 19

(C) 20

(D) 21

14. Which one of the following numbers is prime?

(A) 26

(B) 27

(C) 28

(D) 29

15. Which one of the following numbers is composite?

(A) 67

(B) 69

(C) 71

(D) 73

16. Which one of the following numbers is composite?

(A) 101

(B) 103

(C) 105

(D) 107

17. The number 24 is to be written as a product of its prime factors. Which one of the following is correct?

(A) $24 = 3 \times 8$

(B) $24 = 4 \times 6$

(C) $24 = 2 \times 3 \times 4$

(D) $24 = 2 \times 2 \times 2 \times 3$

18. The number 90 is to be written as a product of its prime factors. Which one of the following is correct?

(A) $90 = 2 \times 5 \times 9$

(B) $90 = 2 \times 3 \times 3 \times 5$

(C) $90 = 3 \times 5 \times 6$

(D) $90 = 2 \times 3 \times 15$

19. The place value of 5 in 780756 is

(A) Five ones

(B) Five tens

(C) 5 tenths

(D) Five hundreds

20. Match the following numbers in list I with the corresponding place value of number 5.

Unit-I	Unit-II
(A) 750	1. 500
(B) 17510	2. 50
(C) 124605	3. 5
(D) 50630	4. 50000

   A B C D   A B C D

(A) 1 2 3 4

(B) 2 1 3 4

(C) 1 2 3 4

(D) 3 1 2 4

21. Adding a number to 22 thousand gives 25 thousands 3 hundreds and 2 tens. The number is _____.
    (A) 3340　　　　　　(B) 3320
    (C) 3680　　　　　　(D) 3660

22. Navneet spends 1.33 hours studying for Computer, 4.67 hours studying for Maths and 0.4 hours studying for Hindi. How much total time does Navneet spends studying?
    (A) Six and four thousandth hour
    (B) Six and four tenths hour
    (C) Six hours
    (D) Six and four hundredth hours

23. Sum of a number of two digits and the number obtained by reversing the digits of the first number is 10 more than 100. If the difference of the digits is 4, then the number is
    (A) 22　　　　　　(B) 64
    (C) 73　　　　　　(D) 81

24. Sum of place values of 6 in 62616 is
    (A) 666　　　　　　(B) 180
    (C) 60606　　　　　　(D) 6006

25. Housing Board built 200 flats. A painter is engaged to serially number each flat individually from 1 to 200. How many times will he be required to write zero?
    (A) 12　　　　　　(B) 18
    (C) 19　　　　　　(D) 22

1.	Ⓐ	Ⓑ	Ⓒ	Ⓓ	6.	Ⓐ	Ⓑ	Ⓒ	Ⓓ	11.	Ⓐ	Ⓑ	Ⓒ	Ⓓ	16.	Ⓐ	Ⓑ	Ⓒ	Ⓓ	21.	Ⓐ	Ⓑ	Ⓒ	Ⓓ
2.	Ⓐ	Ⓑ	Ⓒ	Ⓓ	7.	Ⓐ	Ⓑ	Ⓒ	Ⓓ	12.	Ⓐ	Ⓑ	Ⓒ	Ⓓ	17.	Ⓐ	Ⓑ	Ⓒ	Ⓓ	22.	Ⓐ	Ⓑ	Ⓒ	Ⓓ
3.	Ⓐ	Ⓑ	Ⓒ	Ⓓ	8.	Ⓐ	Ⓑ	Ⓒ	Ⓓ	13.	Ⓐ	Ⓑ	Ⓒ	Ⓓ	18.	Ⓐ	Ⓑ	Ⓒ	Ⓓ	23.	Ⓐ	Ⓑ	Ⓒ	Ⓓ
4.	Ⓐ	Ⓑ	Ⓒ	Ⓓ	9.	Ⓐ	Ⓑ	Ⓒ	Ⓓ	14.	Ⓐ	Ⓑ	Ⓒ	Ⓓ	19.	Ⓐ	Ⓑ	Ⓒ	Ⓓ	24.	Ⓐ	Ⓑ	Ⓒ	Ⓓ
5.	Ⓐ	Ⓑ	Ⓒ	Ⓓ	10.	Ⓐ	Ⓑ	Ⓒ	Ⓓ	15.	Ⓐ	Ⓑ	Ⓒ	Ⓓ	20.	Ⓐ	Ⓑ	Ⓒ	Ⓓ	25.	Ⓐ	Ⓑ	Ⓒ	Ⓓ

COMPUTATION OPERATIONS 

LEARNING OBJECTIVES

- ➤ Rules for writing Roman Numerals
- ➤ Addition
- ➤ Factors
- ➤ How to convert to Roman Numerals
- ➤ Subtraction
- ➤ Common Factors

MULTIPLE CHOICE QUESTIONS

1. The Roman numeral ' CIV' is equal to :
   (A) 108   (B) 44
   (C) 104   (D) 134

2. The Roman numeral ' XLV' is equal to :
   (A) 45   (B) 75
   (C) 12   (D) 66

3. Write 3,396 as a Roman Numeral.
   (A) MMMMMMMCLXXVI
   (B) MMMCXCVI
   (C) MDCXXXVI
   (D) MMMCCCXCVI

4. The Roman numeral 'CXXXIII' is equal to:
   (A) 19   (B) 12
   (C) 133   (D) 17

5. Convert 2,011 to Roman Numerals.
   (A) MCMXI   (B) MMIX
   (C) MMXI   (D) MMXXI

6. Convert 7,192 to Roman Numerals.
   (A) MMMMMMMXCCII
   (B) MMMMMMMCLXXXXII
   (C) MMMMMMCXCII
   (D) MMMMMMMCXCII

7. The Roman numeral ' LXXV' is equal to:
   (A) 66   (B) 45
   (C) 75   (D) 60

8. Write MDCCCXXXVI as a number.
   (A) 2836   (B) 1,836
   (C) 3336   (D) 3836

9. The Roman numeral 'CXXVIII' is equal to:
   (A) 101   (B) 111
   (C) 128   (D) 4

10. The Roman numeral 'IV' is equal to :
    (A) 9   (B) 147
    (C) 4   (D) 110

11. The difference of two numbers is 136452 and the smaller number is 910658. Find the larger number.
    (A) 1047199   (B) 1047110
    (C) 1047201   (D) 104700

12. Multiply 4132 × 27.
    (A) 115464   (B) 111564
    (C) 111574   (D) 1111584

13. Multiply 81.009 × 8989
    (A) 728189.901   (B) 728188.901
    (C) 728189.911   (D) 7281.89901

14. Find the quotient 618974 ÷ 56
    (A) 11053   (B) 11052
    (C) 11051   (D) 11000

15. Find the remainder 806873 ÷ 637
    (A) 431   (B) 298
    (C) 196   (D) 493

16. Simplify (15 × 3) ÷ 5 × 8 – 2 + 6 × (8 – 2)
    (A) 96   (B) 106
    (C) 86   (D) 56

17. Simplify the following and check
    (i) 12 × 6 ÷ 3 and; (ii) 12 × (6 ÷ 3)
    (A) (i) > (ii)   (B) (i) < (ii)
    (C) (i) = (ii)   (D) None of these

18. A factory produces 13780 bulbs everyday. How many bulbs will be produced in 278 days?
    (A) 3830824   (B) 3830840
    (C) 3830480   (D) 3830400

19. Divide the greatest number of 9 digits by the greatest number of 3 digits.
    (A) 1001001   (B) 1001101
    (C) 1001011   (D) 1000001

20. The product of two numbers is 127008. One of them is 882. Find the other number.
    (A) 144   (B) 124
    (C) 444   (D) 134

21. Find the greatest number that will divide 43, 91 and 183 so as to leave the same remainder in each case.
    (A) 4   (B) 77
    (C) 9   (D) 13

22. What is a factor?
    (A) A number that divides exactly into another number.
    (B) A number that can be halved.
    (C) A number that can be multiplied by itself.
    (D) A number that can be divided only by two.

23. The H.C.F. of two numbers is 23 and the other two factors of their L.C.M. are 13 and 14. The larger of the two numbers is :
    (A) 276   (B) 299
    (C) 322   (D) 345

24. Which numbers are all factors of 10?
    (A) 2, 3, 5   (B) 1, 2, 4
    (C) 2, 5, 10   (D) All of these

25. Which numbers are all factors of 16?
    (A) 4, 6, 8.   (B) 2, 8, 4.
    (C) 1, 2, 9.   (D) All of these

26. Which number is a multiple of 2?
    (A) 1321   (B) 2543
    (C) 5620   (D) 1211

27. Let N be the greatest number that will divide 1305, 4665 and 6905, leaving the same remainder in each case. Then sum of the digits in N is :
    (A) 4   (B) 5
    (C) 6   (D) 8

28. Which number is a multiple of 5?
    (A) 2876   (B) 1985
    (C) 1423   (D) 1202

29. Which pair of factors makes 20?
    (A) 2 and 18   (B) 15 and 5
    (C) 4 and 5   (D) 2 and 7

30. What is the least common multiple of 6 and 8?
    (A) 12   (B) 16
    (C) 24   (D) 48

31. **Statement A:** C = 25.
    Statement B: M > 100.
    (A) Statement A is true.
    (B) Statement B is false.
    (C) Both statements are true.
    (D) Only statement B is true.

32. **Statement A:** In Roman numerals system, the symbol VC does not represent the number 95.
    Statement B: The ascending order of numbers X, VI, VII, IX is X, IX, VI, VII.
    (A) Only B is true   (B) Only A is true
    (C) Both are true   (D) None of these

33. Kavita Mehra is XII years old. Her brother is X years old. How old will they be when their total age is L years?
    (A) XXIX, XXVI   (B) XXVI, XXIV
    (C) XX, XXIII   (D) XIX, XXII

34. Select the correct Roman numerals in Column I with Hindu-Arabic numerals in Column II.

Column I	Column II
(A) CCXVIII	318
(B) DCCLXIX	769
(C) MMMCCXCIX	3399
(D) VDCCXLVII	5748

35. What will be the outcome for the given diagram?

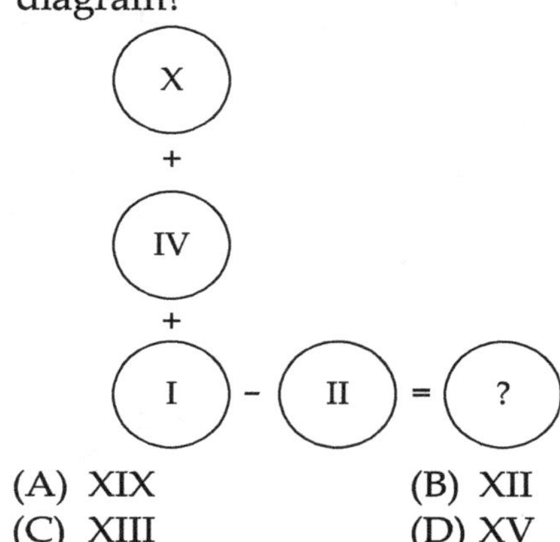

(A) XIX   (B) XII
(C) XIII   (D) XV

Darken Your Choice with HB Pencil

1.	Ⓐ Ⓑ Ⓒ Ⓓ	8.	Ⓐ Ⓑ Ⓒ Ⓓ	15.	Ⓐ Ⓑ Ⓒ Ⓓ	22	Ⓐ Ⓑ Ⓒ Ⓓ	29.	Ⓐ Ⓑ Ⓒ Ⓓ
2.	Ⓐ Ⓑ Ⓒ Ⓓ	9.	Ⓐ Ⓑ Ⓒ Ⓓ	16.	Ⓐ Ⓑ Ⓒ Ⓓ	23.	Ⓐ Ⓑ Ⓒ Ⓓ	30.	Ⓐ Ⓑ Ⓒ Ⓓ
3.	Ⓐ Ⓑ Ⓒ Ⓓ	10.	Ⓐ Ⓑ Ⓒ Ⓓ	17.	Ⓐ Ⓑ Ⓒ Ⓓ	24.	Ⓐ Ⓑ Ⓒ Ⓓ	31.	Ⓐ Ⓑ Ⓒ Ⓓ
4.	Ⓐ Ⓑ Ⓒ Ⓓ	11.	Ⓐ Ⓑ Ⓒ Ⓓ	18.	Ⓐ Ⓑ Ⓒ Ⓓ	25.	Ⓐ Ⓑ Ⓒ Ⓓ	32.	Ⓐ Ⓑ Ⓒ Ⓓ
5.	Ⓐ Ⓑ Ⓒ Ⓓ	12.	Ⓐ Ⓑ Ⓒ Ⓓ	19.	Ⓐ Ⓑ Ⓒ Ⓓ	26.	Ⓐ Ⓑ Ⓒ Ⓓ	33.	Ⓐ Ⓑ Ⓒ Ⓓ
6.	Ⓐ Ⓑ Ⓒ Ⓓ	13.	Ⓐ Ⓑ Ⓒ Ⓓ	20.	Ⓐ Ⓑ Ⓒ Ⓓ	27.	Ⓐ Ⓑ Ⓒ Ⓓ	34.	Ⓐ Ⓑ Ⓒ Ⓓ
7.	Ⓐ Ⓑ Ⓒ Ⓓ	14.	Ⓐ Ⓑ Ⓒ Ⓓ	21.	Ⓐ Ⓑ Ⓒ Ⓓ	28.	Ⓐ Ⓑ Ⓒ Ⓓ	35.	Ⓐ Ⓑ Ⓒ Ⓓ

DECIMALS AND FRACTIONS 

LEARNING OBJECTIVES

- ➤ Decimal Point
- ➤ Equivalent Fractions
- ➤ Adding and Subtracting Decimals
- ➤ Comparing Fractions

MULTIPLE CHOICE QUESTIONS

1. Which of the following is equal to twenty-five and sixty-nine thousandths?
   (A) 25.069
   (B) 25.0690
   (C) 25.06900
   (D) All of the above

2. The number 32747 written to 4 significant figures is
   (A) 32740
   (B) 32750
   (C) 3274
   (D) 32752

3. Which of the following is equal to seven hundred and five thousand and eighty-nine ten-thousandths?
   (A) 700.005.089
   (B) 705,000.089
   (C) 705,000.0089
   (D) 705,000.00089

4. Which of the following is equal to 9,842.1039?
   (A) Nine thousand, eight hundred, forty two and one thousand, thirty-nine millionths
   (B) Nine thousand, eight hundred, forty-two and one thousand, thirty-nine ten-thousandths
   (C) Nine thousand, eight hundred, forty-two and one thousand, thirty-nine thousandths
   (D) None of the above

5. Which of the following is equal to five hundred-thousandths?
   (A) 500,000
   (B) 0.500
   (C) 0.0005
   (D) 0.00005

6. Which of the following is the smallest decimal number?
   (A) 0.4981
   (B) 0.52
   (C) 0.4891
   (D) 0.6

7. What is the hundredths digit in the number 356.812?
   (A) 1
   (B) 2
   (C) 3
   (D) 8

8. For the decimal number 83.72 what is the digit in the hundredths place?
   (A) 2
   (B) 3
   (C) 7
   (D) 8

9. Which of the following choices lists these decimals in order from least to greatest : 0.910, 0.091, 0.9?
   (A) 0.9, 0.091, 0.910
   (B) 0.910, 0.9, 0.091
   (C) 0.091, 0.9, 0.910
   (D) None of the Above

10. Which of the following choices lists these decimals in order from least to greatest : 3.45, 3.0459, 3.5, 3.4059?

   (A) 3.0459, 3.4059, 3.45, 3.5
   (B) 3.4059, 3.5, 3.0459, 3.45
   (C) 3.5, 3.45, 3.4059, 3.0459
   (D) None of the above

11. $(0.1 + 0.01)(0.1 - 0.01) =$

   (A) 0.0001   (B) 0.001
   (C) 0.009   (D) 0.0099

12. For the number 489.6327, where do you find the smallest digit?

   (A) In the hundreds place
   (B) In the hundredths place
   (C) In the thousandths place
   (D) In the ten-thousandths place

13. Which of the following choices lists these decimals in order from least to greatest : 7.102, 7.0102, 7.012, 7.00102, 7.102021?

   (A) 7.102021, 7.00102, 7.012, 7.0102, 7.102
   (B) 7.00102, 7.0102, 7.012, 7.102, 7.102021
   (C) 7.102021, 7.102, 7.012, 7.0102, 7.00102
   (D) None of the above

14. What is the number obtained when 2.0837 is rounded to 2 decimal places?

   (A) 2.09   (B) 2.08
   (C) 2.1   (D) 2.10

15. For the number 36.2495, what is the place value of the digit 9?

   (A) 9 tenths
   (B) 9 hundredths
   (C) 9 thousandths
   (D) 9 ten-thousandths

16. What is the tenths digit in the number 43.765?

   (A) 7   (B) 6
   (C) 5   (D) 4

17. Add 20.15, 0.083 and 6.9

   (A) 27.133   (B) 27.033
   (C) 27.88   (D) 9.133

18. Add 3.032, 7.89 and 103.2

   (A) 114.41   (B) 114.122
   (C) 113.609   (D) 24.122

19. For the number 25.639, what is the place value of the digit 6?

   (A) 6 tens   (B) 6 units
   (C) 6 tenths   (D) 6 hundredths

20. For the number 2,367.981, where do you find the largest digit?

   (A) In the thousands place
   (B) In the units place
   (C) In the tenths place
   (D) In the hundredths place

21. How much pizza is left on the plate?

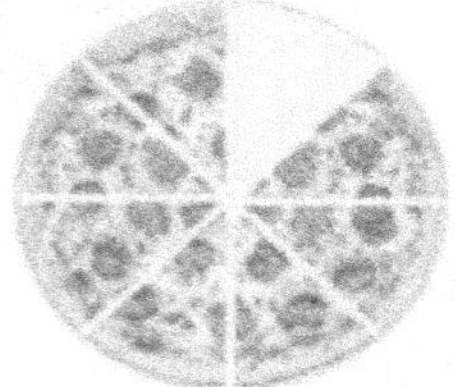

   (A) $\dfrac{8}{7}$ (B) $\dfrac{5}{8}$

   (C) $\dfrac{3}{4}$ (D) $\dfrac{7}{8}$

22. For the fraction of pizza shown in the diagram, what is the numerator?

   (A) 3   (B) 4
   (C) 5   (D) 8

23. What fraction has denominator 12 and equivalent to 2/3.

   (A) $\dfrac{8}{12}$ (B) $\dfrac{9}{12}$

   (C) $\dfrac{11}{12}$ (D) $\dfrac{7}{2} = \dfrac{49}{14}$

24. Which one of the following fractions is NOT equivalent to all the others?

(A) $\dfrac{4}{10}$

(B) $\dfrac{6}{15}$

(C) $\dfrac{9}{20}$

(D) $\dfrac{32}{80}$

25. Which of the following can be written in the box $\dfrac{7}{2} = \dfrac{49}{\Box}$

(A) 16

(B) 14

(C) 28

(D) 35

HOTS (ACHIEVERS SECTION)

26. Which of the following holds true or false?

A. $0.2 = 0.2000$

B. $0.2 = \dfrac{2}{100}$

C. $0.2 = 2 \times \dfrac{1}{1000}$

D. $0.2 = 2.0$

(A) FTFF

(B) TFFF

(C) FFTF

(D) FFFT

27. A cook buys 4 kg of wheat and 3.5 kg of pulses for making the dinner for his customers and uses 2.5 kg of wheat and 1.5 kg of pulses in the dinner. What is the amount of wheat and pulses left with him?

(A) 1.5 kg, 2.75 kg

(B) 2.5 kg, 2 kg

(C) 2.25 kg, 1.75 kg

(D) 1.5 kg, 2 kg

28. The sum $0.5 + 0.75 = 1.25$ can be expressed using fractions as:

(A) $1/2 + 3/5 = 4/3$

(B) $1/2 + 3/4 = 5/4$

(C) $1/2 + 3/7 = 5/8$

(D) $1/2 + 7/3 = 2/7$

29. Electricity bill of Mr. Bunny Mehra shows the following details:

Monthly Rent = 500/–

Unit	Consumed Rate
1-100	3.50
101-150	4.25
151-200	4.50
greater than 201	4.75

Calculate amount payable by Bunny to UPPCL if he consumes 124 units.

(A) 935

(B) 952

(C) 953

(D) 630

30. Find the value of $624.7 + 39.29$.

(A) 101.76

(B) 663.99

(C) 66.399

(D) 660.79

1.	Ⓐ Ⓑ Ⓒ Ⓓ	7.	Ⓐ Ⓑ Ⓒ Ⓓ	13.	Ⓐ Ⓑ Ⓒ Ⓓ	19	Ⓐ Ⓑ Ⓒ Ⓓ	25.	Ⓐ Ⓑ Ⓒ Ⓓ
2.	Ⓐ Ⓑ Ⓒ Ⓓ	8.	Ⓐ Ⓑ Ⓒ Ⓓ	14.	Ⓐ Ⓑ Ⓒ Ⓓ	20.	Ⓐ Ⓑ Ⓒ Ⓓ	26.	Ⓐ Ⓑ Ⓒ Ⓓ
3.	Ⓐ Ⓑ Ⓒ Ⓓ	9.	Ⓐ Ⓑ Ⓒ Ⓓ	15.	Ⓐ Ⓑ Ⓒ Ⓓ	21.	Ⓐ Ⓑ Ⓒ Ⓓ	27.	Ⓐ Ⓑ Ⓒ Ⓓ
4.	Ⓐ Ⓑ Ⓒ Ⓓ	10.	Ⓐ Ⓑ Ⓒ Ⓓ	16.	Ⓐ Ⓑ Ⓒ Ⓓ	22.	Ⓐ Ⓑ Ⓒ Ⓓ	28.	Ⓐ Ⓑ Ⓒ Ⓓ
5.	Ⓐ Ⓑ Ⓒ Ⓓ	11.	Ⓐ Ⓑ Ⓒ Ⓓ	17.	Ⓐ Ⓑ Ⓒ Ⓓ	23.	Ⓐ Ⓑ Ⓒ Ⓓ	29.	Ⓐ Ⓑ Ⓒ Ⓓ
6.	Ⓐ Ⓑ Ⓒ Ⓓ	12.	Ⓐ Ⓑ Ⓒ Ⓓ	18.	Ⓐ Ⓑ Ⓒ Ⓓ	24.	Ⓐ Ⓑ Ⓒ Ⓓ	30.	Ⓐ Ⓑ Ⓒ Ⓓ

MEASUREMENTS

LEARNING OBJECTIVES

➤ Length
➤ Temperature
➤ Unit of Currency in India

➤ Volume
➤ Conversions
➤ Misconception/Fact

➤ Weight
➤ Thermometer

MULTIPLE CHOICE QUESTIONS

1. To convert minutes into seconds we multiply the number of minutes by
   (A) 70　　　　　　(B) 60
   (C) 30　　　　　　(D) 50

2. The time from 12'O clock noon to 12'O clock mid-night is called.
   (A) am　　　　　　(B) pm
   (C) both (A) and (B)　(D) none of these

3. The number of seconds in 7 minutes is
   (A) 400 sec　　　　(B) 320 sec
   (C) 420 sec　　　　(D) 460 sec

4. The time from 12'O clock midnight to 12'O clock-noon is
   (A) am　　　　　　(B) pm
   (C) both (A) and (B)　(D) None of these

5. The number of seconds in 5 minutes is
   (A) 400 sec　　　　(B) 500 sec
   (C) 100 sec　　　　(D) 300 sec

6. To convert hours into seconds, we multiply the number of hours by
   (A) 60　　　　　　(B) 1200
   (C) 3600　　　　　(D) 300'

7. To convert hours into minutes, we multiply the number of hours by
   (A) 60　　　　　　(B) 120
   (C) 360　　　　　(D) 120

8. To convert days into hours we multiply the no. of days by
   (A) 20　　　　　　(B) 30
   (C) 24　　　　　　(D) 31

9. The number of days in the month of February in a leap year is
   (A) 30　　　　　　(B) 29
   (C) 31　　　　　　(D) All of them

10. To convert seconds into minutes we divide the number of seconds by
    (A) 60　　　　　　(B) 120
    (C) 30　　　　　　(D) None of these

11. Ten celsius equals _Fahrenhiet.
    (A) 20°　　　　　(B) 30°
    (C) 40°　　　　　(D) 50°

12. Convert 32° Celsius to Fahrenheit.
    (A) 100°F　　　　(B) 89.6°F
    (C) 57.6°F　　　　(D) 0°F

13. Eighty Fahrenheit is _ Celsius.
    (A) 17°　　　　　(B) 27°
    (C) 37°　　　　　(D) 47°

14. Which is the formula to convert Celsius to Fahrenheit?
    (A) $T_f = 1.8 \times T_c + 52$
    (B) $T_f = 1.8 \times T_c + 42$
    (C) $T_f = 1.8 \times T_c + 32$
    (D) None of these

15. Convert 11° Celsius to Fahrenheit.
    (A) 51.8°F   (B) 19.8°F
    (C) 6.11°F   (D) –11.67°F

16. Convert 68° Fahrenheit to Celsius.
    (A) 154.4°C   (B) 64.8°C
    (C) 55.6°C   (D) 20°C

17. Convert 18° Fahrenheit to Celsius.
    (A) –25.2°C   (B) –7.8°C
    (C) 7.8°C   (D) 64.4°C

18. The highest temperature ever recorded on Earth was 57.8°C, in Libya, Africa in 1922. How many degrees Fahrenheit was this, to the nearest degree?
    (A) 14°F   (B) 104°F
    (C) 136°F   (D) 140°F

19. The highest temperature ever recorded in the UK was 101.3°F, recorded in Kent in 2003. How many degrees Celsius was this?
    (A) 38.5°C   (B) 39.5°C
    (C) 56.3°C   (D) 214.3°C

20. Convert 41° Fahrenheit to Celsius:
    (A) 5 °C   (B) – 25.2°C
    (C) – 5 °C   (D) 7.8°C

21. Golu went to purchase cricket kit and gave two coins of ₹ 5, four notes of ₹ 10, three notes of ₹ 50 and two notes of ₹ 500 to cashier. If the price of cricket kit was ₹ 1162, the change that he would have got back is __________.
    (A) ₹ 38   (B) ₹ 15
    (C) ₹ 30   (D) ₹ 32

22. Kapil bought 5 cookies all having equal price. If the total amount paid is ₹ 33, what was the price of one cookie?

    (A) ₹ 5   (B) ₹ 5.50
    (C) ₹ 6.00   (D) ₹ 6.60

Direction (23-27) : Consider the prices of these items below to answer questions.

    Apple _________ ₹ 180 per kg
    Pen _________ ₹ 8 per piece
    Eraser _________ ₹ 5 for 2 erasers
    Chocolates _________ ₹ 15 for 3 chocolates

23. Ankit wants to buy half kg apples and one chocolate. The total amount he needs to pay is :
    (A) ₹ 85   (B) ₹ 95
    (C) ₹ 90   (D) ₹ 105

24. If Bunny wants to buy one pen and 3 erasers, how much he needs to pay?
    (A) ₹ 13   (B) ₹ 15
    (C) ₹ 15.50   (D) ₹ 16.25

25. One kg apples can be bought for ₹ 180 and two chocolates can be bought for ₹ 7.50. This statement is __________.
    (A) True
    (B) False
    (C) Insufficient information
    (D) None of these

26. If Manpreet has ₹ 122 and he wants to buy as many chocolates he can with this amount, the number of chocolates that he can buy is:
    (A) 15   (B) 20
    (C) 24   (D) 30

27. Which of the following statement is false?
    (A) Cost of (one kg apples + 2 pens) > Cost of (half kg apples + 5 pens)
    (B) Cost of 5 erasers > Cost of 2 chocolates.
    (C) Cost of 6 erasers > Cost of 3 chocolates.
    (D) Cost of (half kg apples +2 pen +1 erasers) > Cost of 9 chocolates

28. Yuvraj is very fond of reading books. Once he bought books for ₹ 465 and he paid ₹ 500 to the bookstore, which expression shows the correct amount of change that he will get back?

(A) ₹ 500 + ₹ 465   (B) ₹ 500 – ₹ 465

(C) ₹ 500 ÷ ₹ 465   (D) ₹ 500 × ₹ 465

Direction (29-30) : Consider the following scenario to answer questions.

Shraddha and Shubhra are two friends and one day they decided to go for shopping together. Shraddha had ₹ 1500 and Shubhra had ₹ 2000 with them. Shraddha purchased shoes for ₹ 550, a skirt for ₹ 275 and movie DVD for ₹ 50. Shubhra purchased top for ₹ 250, a bag for ₹ 480, a book for ₹ 115 and a tennis racket for ₹ 500.

29. What is the total money spent by Shraddha and Shubhra together in shopping?

(A) ₹ 2220   (B) ₹ 2170

(C) ₹ 1720   (D) ₹ 880

30. The amount left with Shubhra after shopping is __________.

(A) ₹ 540   (B) ₹ 550

(C) ₹ 555   (D) ₹ 655

HOTS (ACHIEVERS SECTION)

31. Shubhra participated in a race. She took 1 hour 36 minutes and 14 seconds to complete the race. How many seconds did she take to complete the race?

(A) 2220 seconds   (B) 2234 seconds

(C) 5760 seconds   (D) 5774 seconds

32. Praveen bought 5 tins of orange juice each containing 0.75 litre of orange juice. He poured the orange juice into a 6−litre container. How many more tins must Praveen buy to fill up the container with orange juice?

(A) 30   (B) 2

(C) 5   (D) 3

33. The ratio of Anita's mass to Mamata's mass is 4:7. If their total mass is 99 kg, what is Mamata's mass?

(A) 63 kg   (B) 45 kg

(C) 36 kg   (D) 54 kg

34. Choose the correct option.

(A) 95°C = 105°F   (B) 60°C = 120°F

(C) 33°C = 95°F   (D) 75°C = 167°F

35. The price of a watch is ₹ 982.75. How much money will be needed to buy 46 such watches?

(A) ₹ 45106.50   (B) ₹ 45206.50

(C) ₹ 45000.50   (D) ₹ 45200.00

—Darken Your Choice with HB Pencil—

1.	Ⓐ Ⓑ Ⓒ Ⓓ	8.	Ⓐ Ⓑ Ⓒ Ⓓ	15.	Ⓐ Ⓑ Ⓒ Ⓓ	22	Ⓐ Ⓑ Ⓒ Ⓓ	29.	Ⓐ Ⓑ Ⓒ Ⓓ
2.	Ⓐ Ⓑ Ⓒ Ⓓ	9.	Ⓐ Ⓑ Ⓒ Ⓓ	16.	Ⓐ Ⓑ Ⓒ Ⓓ	23.	Ⓐ Ⓑ Ⓒ Ⓓ	30.	Ⓐ Ⓑ Ⓒ Ⓓ
3.	Ⓐ Ⓑ Ⓒ Ⓓ	10.	Ⓐ Ⓑ Ⓒ Ⓓ	17.	Ⓐ Ⓑ Ⓒ Ⓓ	24.	Ⓐ Ⓑ Ⓒ Ⓓ	31.	Ⓐ Ⓑ Ⓒ Ⓓ
4.	Ⓐ Ⓑ Ⓒ Ⓓ	11.	Ⓐ Ⓑ Ⓒ Ⓓ	18.	Ⓐ Ⓑ Ⓒ Ⓓ	25.	Ⓐ Ⓑ Ⓒ Ⓓ	32.	Ⓐ Ⓑ Ⓒ Ⓓ
5.	Ⓐ Ⓑ Ⓒ Ⓓ	12.	Ⓐ Ⓑ Ⓒ Ⓓ	19.	Ⓐ Ⓑ Ⓒ Ⓓ	26.	Ⓐ Ⓑ Ⓒ Ⓓ	33.	Ⓐ Ⓑ Ⓒ Ⓓ
6.	Ⓐ Ⓑ Ⓒ Ⓓ	13.	Ⓐ Ⓑ Ⓒ Ⓓ	20.	Ⓐ Ⓑ Ⓒ Ⓓ	27.	Ⓐ Ⓑ Ⓒ Ⓓ	34.	Ⓐ Ⓑ Ⓒ Ⓓ
7.	Ⓐ Ⓑ Ⓒ Ⓓ	14.	Ⓐ Ⓑ Ⓒ Ⓓ	21.	Ⓐ Ⓑ Ⓒ Ⓓ	28.	Ⓐ Ⓑ Ⓒ Ⓓ	35.	Ⓐ Ⓑ Ⓒ Ⓓ

ALGEBRA

LEARNING OBJECTIVES

➤ Basic concepts of Algebra

MULTIPLE CHOICE QUESTIONS

1. Two times b – six times a =
   (A) $2b - 6a$ (B) $6b - 2a$
   (C) $b - 2a$ (D) $b^2 - a6$

2. Sum of twice of x and 6 =
   (A) $6x + 2$ (B) $2x + 6$
   (C) $x + 8$ (D) $2(x + 6)$

3. Sum of n and 20 =
   (A) $n + 20$ (B) $20 - n$
   (C) $20n$ (D) $6 + 14n$

4. Three times x minus five times x =
   (A) $3x - 5y$ (B) $5x - 3x$
   (C) $x - 3y$ (D) $3x - 5x$

5. Twice the sum of d and e
   (A) $d + 2e$ (B) $2d + e$
   (C) $2(d + e)$ (D) $2de$

6. The quotient when twice x is divided by thrice y
   (A) $2x/y$ (B) $2x/3y$
   (C) $2x/4y$ (D) $3x/2y$

7. If $x = 2, y = 5$ then $x + y = ?$
   (A) 12   (B) 10
   (C) 3   (D) 7

8. If $x = 6, y = 2$ then $x - y = ?$
   (A) 4   (B) 3
   (C) 5   (D) 12

9. If $m = 5, n = 4$ then $mn = ?$
   (A) 12   (B) 15
   (C) 20   (D) 24

10. If $p = 1/6, q = 20$ then $p \times q = ?$
    (A) 5/3   (B) 5/6
    (C) 10/3   (D) None of these

11. If $p = 28, q = 7$ then $p/q = ?$
    (A) 3   (B) 12
    (C) 6   (D) 4

12. If $x = 50, y = 5$ then $x/y = ?$
    (A) 5   (B) 10
    (C) 12   (D) 8

13. If $a = 10, b = 3$, then $a - b = ?$
    (A) 13   (B) 7
    (C) 4   (D) 45

14. If $x + 5 = 10$, then x represents _______.
    (A) known number
    (B) unknown number
    (C) none of these

15. In $x + 3$, x is known as
    (A) variable   (B) none of these
    (C) constant   (D) alphabet

16. If $a = 9$, $b = 3$ then $a^2 \div b - a = ?$
    - (A) 3
    - (B) 9
    - (C) 18
    - (D) 15

17. If $a = 5$, $b = 2$ then $a^2 + b^2 - ab^3 = ?$
    - (A) −11
    - (B) −9
    - (C) −12
    - (D) −15

18. If $a = 2$, $b = 3$, $c = 4$ then $a^2 b - c = ?$
    - (A) 3
    - (B) 8
    - (C) 10
    - (D) 5

19. If $a = 5$, $b = 4$ then $a^2 \div (b + 1) = ?$
    - (A) 2
    - (B) 18
    - (C) 5
    - (D) 20

20. If $a = 30$, $b = 20$, $c = 40$ then $b^2 - a + c = ?$
    - (A) 300
    - (B) 410
    - (C) 180
    - (D) 250

Darken Your Choice with HB Pencil

1.	A B C D	5.	A B C D	9.	A B C D	13	A B C D	17.	A B C D
2.	A B C D	6.	A B C D	10.	A B C D	14.	A B C D	18.	A B C D
3.	A B C D	7.	A B C D	11.	A B C D	15.	A B C D	19.	A B C D
4.	A B C D	8.	A B C D	12.	A B C D	16.	A B C D	20.	A B C D

GEOMETRICAL SHAPES AND ANGLES

LEARNING OBJECTIVES

- ➤ Geometry
- ➤ Labeling Angles
- ➤ Parts of triangles
- ➤ Types of triangles
- ➤ Reflection Symmetry
- ➤ Rotational Symmetry

MULTIPLE CHOICE QUESTIONS

1. By using the three letters on the shape that define the angle, angle α is written as:

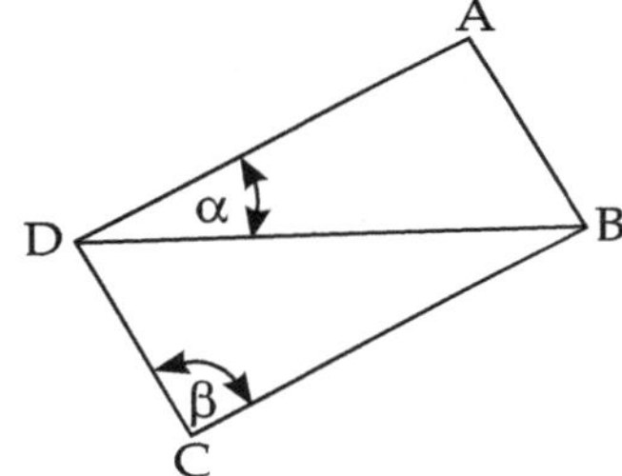

   (A) ∠ABD   (B) ∠ADB
   (C) ∠BAD   (D) ∠BDC

2. By using the three letters on the shape that define the angle, angle β is written as:

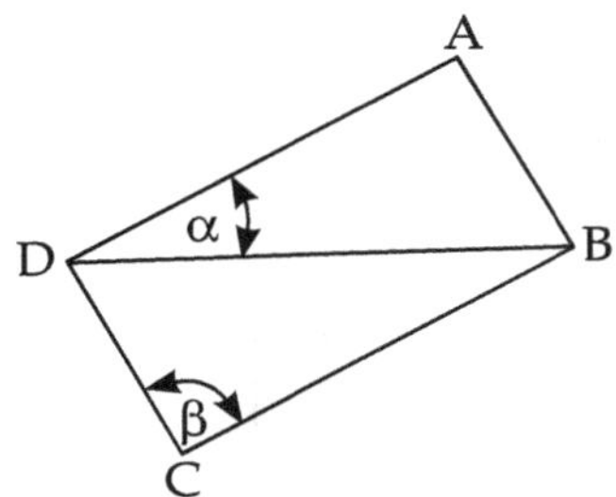

   (A) ∠DCB   (B) ∠BDC
   (C) ∠CBD   (D) ∠ACB

3. If two acute angles are added together, which of the following is NOT possible for their sum :
   - (A) Acute
   - (B) Right
   - (C) Obtuse
   - (D) Straight

4. Which one of the following angles is acute?
   - (A) Half a right angle
   - (B) A right angle
   - (C) One and a half right angles
   - (D) Two right angles

5. How many acute angles are there in the diagram?

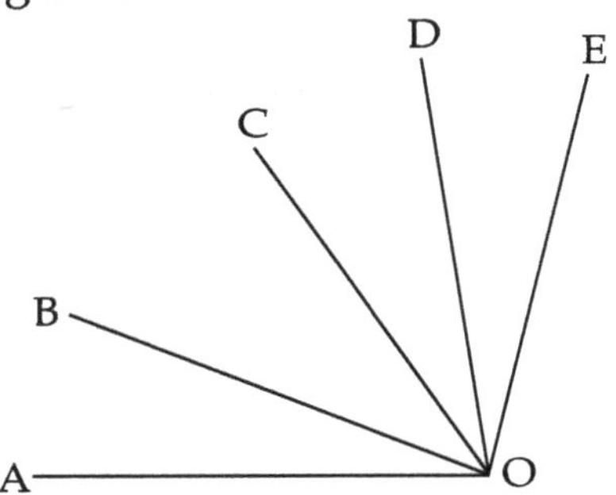

   (Think of all possibilities).
   (A) 10   (B) 9
   (C) 7   (D) 4

6. How many acute angles are there in this pentagram?

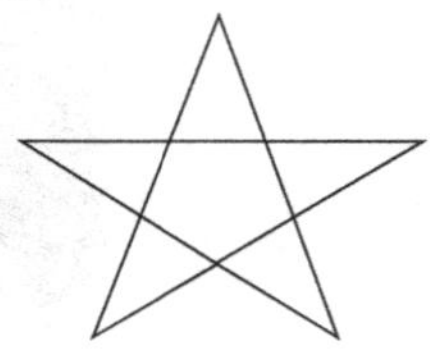

(A) 5   (B) 10
(C) 15   (D) 20

7. How many acute angles are there in the diagram?

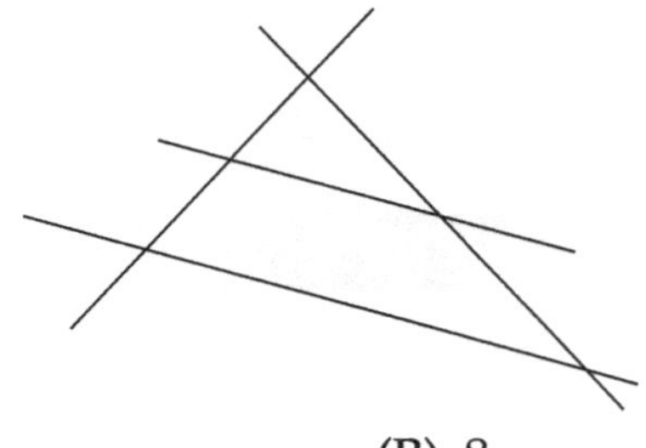

(A) 5   (B) 8
(C) 9   (D) 10

8. How many acute angles are there in the diagram?

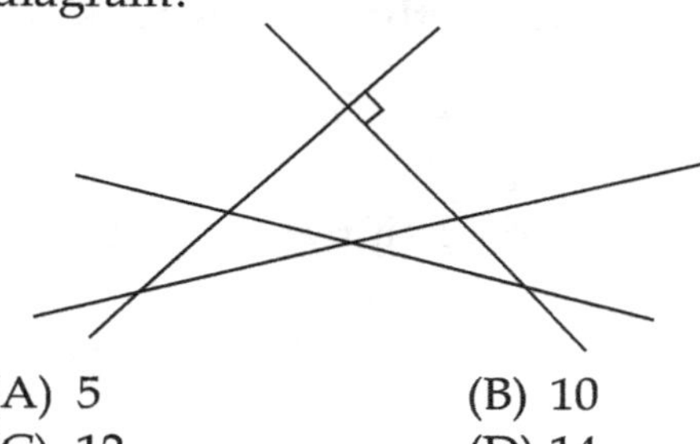

(A) 5   (B) 10
(C) 12   (D) 14

9. How many right angles are there in the diagram?

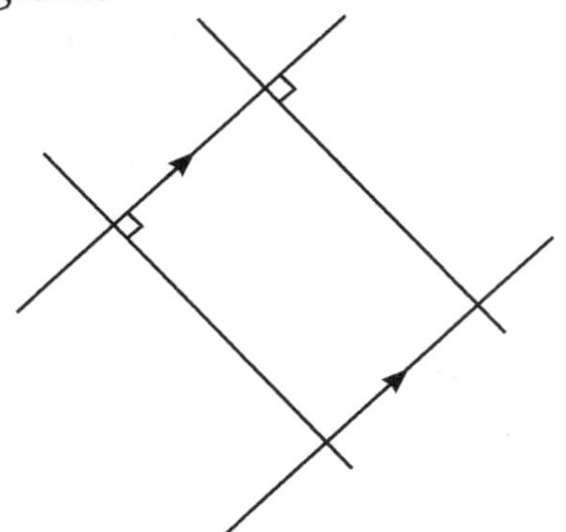

10. How many right angles make two full rotations?

(A) 2   (B) 4
(C) 8   (D) 16

10. How many right angles make two full rotations?

(A) 4   (B) 6
(C) 8   (D) 10

11. How many obtuse angles are there in the diagram?

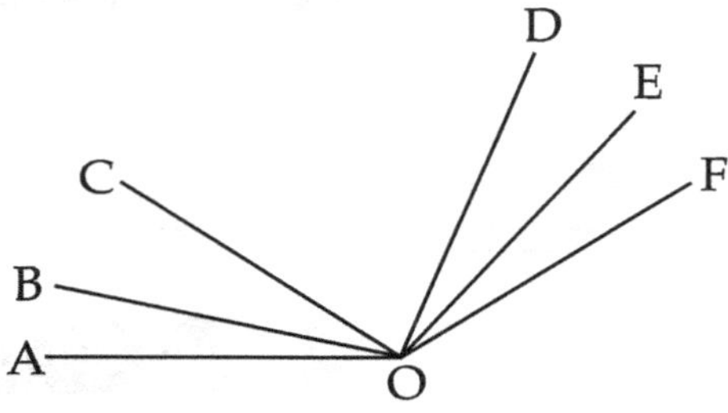

(A) 7   (B) 8
(C) 9   (D) 10

12. Which one of the following angles is obtuse?

(A) Half a right angle
(B) One right angle
(C) One and a half right angles
(D) Two right angles

13. How many straight angles are there in three full rotations?

(A) 3   (B) 4
(C) 6   (D) 8

14. Which one of the following angles is not reflex?

(A) 178°   (B) 182°
(C) 270°   (D) 359°

15. Which one of the following angles is reflex?

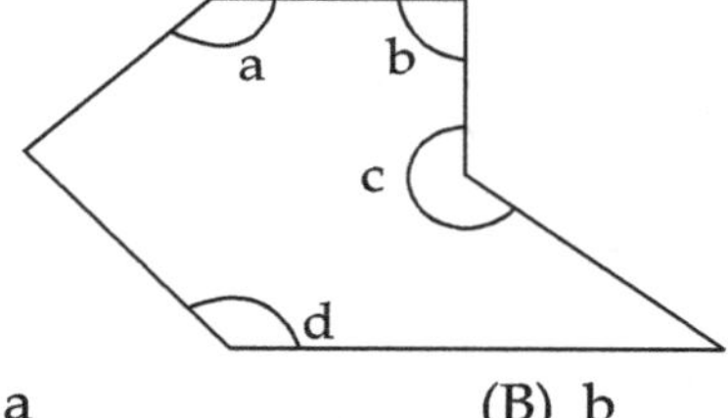

(A) a   (B) b
(C) c   (D) d

16. If angle AOB = 67°, what is the size of reflex angle AOB?

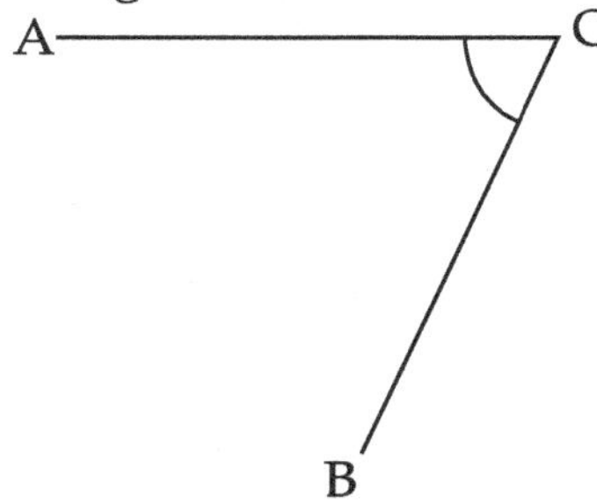

(A) 113°   (B) 247°
(C) 293°   (D) 427°

17. What is the least number of 33° angles you would need to make a reflex angle?

(A) 2   (B) 5
(C) 6   (D) 7

18. Which of the following describes the triangle shown above?

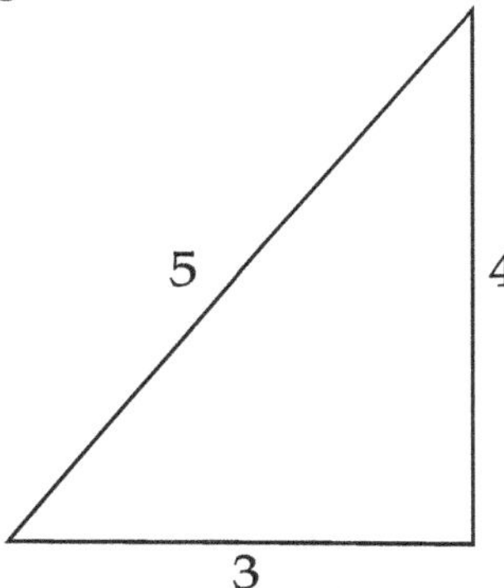

(A) A scalene right angled triangle
(B) A scalene obtuse angled triangle
(C) A scalene acute angled triangle
(D) An isosceles right angled triangle

19. A triangle is isosceles and right angled. Which of the following statements must be false?

(A) The triangle has angles 45°, 45° and 90°
(B) The triangle has two of its sides equal
(C) The triangle has one line of symmetry
(D) The triangle has sides of lengths 3, 4 and 5

20. Shraddha made two copies of the right angled triangle shown and cut them out.

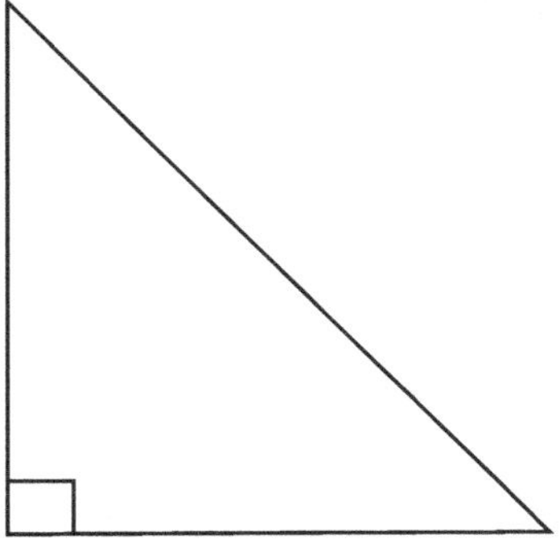

She then joined edges of the triangles together to make shapes. Which of the following shapes was not possible for Shraddha to make?

(A) A square
(B) A kite
(C) A parallelogram
(D) An isosceles triangle

21. Shraddha made two copies of the following isosceles right angled triangle and cut them out. She then joined edges of the triangles together to make shapes.

Which of the following shapes was it NOT possible for Shraddha to make?

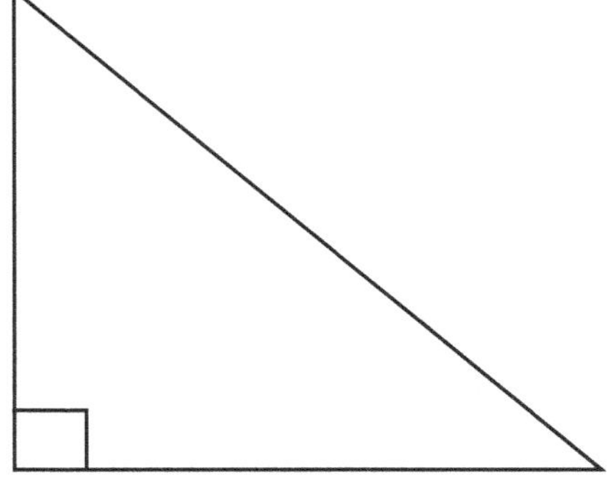

(A) A square
(B) An equilateral triangle
(C) A parallelogram
(D) An isosceles triangle

22. The square is turned one complete rotation about the point O. Which of the rotation following shows the new position of the square?

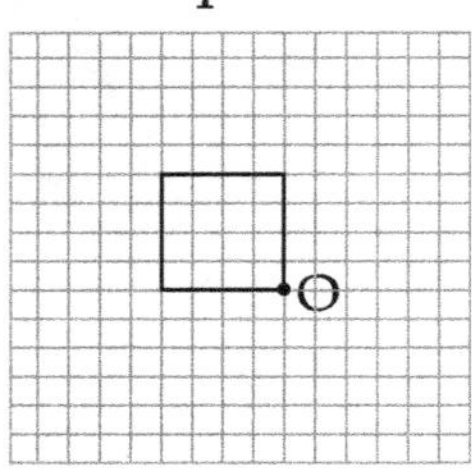

(A) 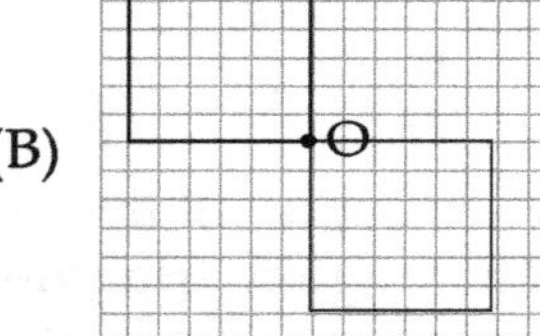

(B) 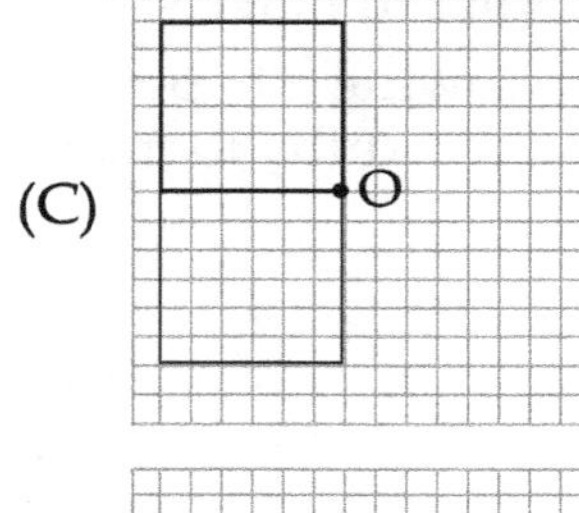

(C) 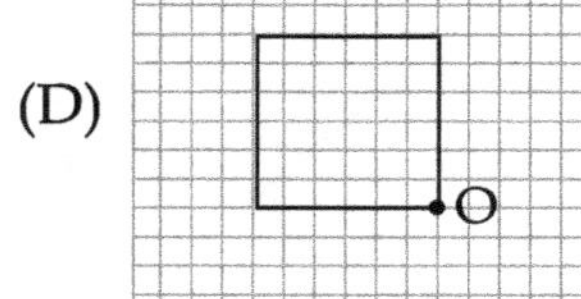

(D)

23. How many lines of symmetry does this star have?

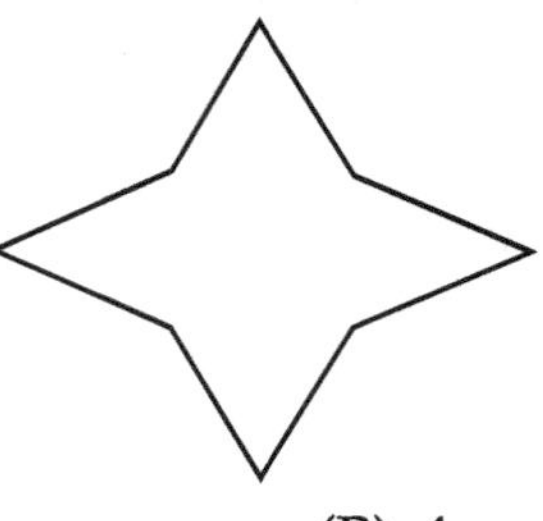

(A) 2   (B) 4
(C) 6   (D) 8

24. What is the order of rotational symmetry of this star?

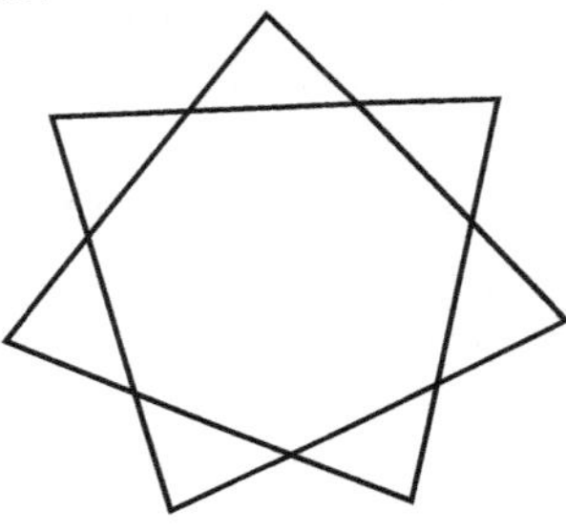

(A) 5   (B) 6
(C) 7   (D) 8

25. What is the order of rotational symmetry of this shape?

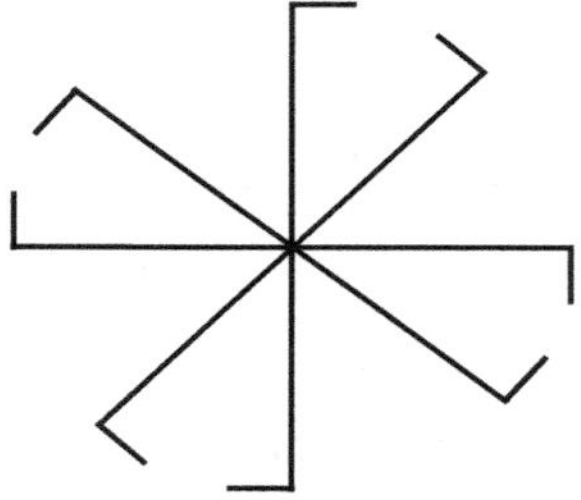

(A) 2   (B) 4
(C) 8   (D) 16

26. Which figure has no line of symmetry?

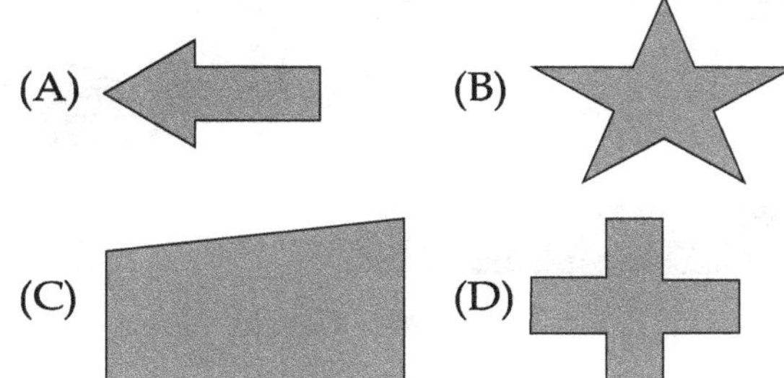

(A) (B)

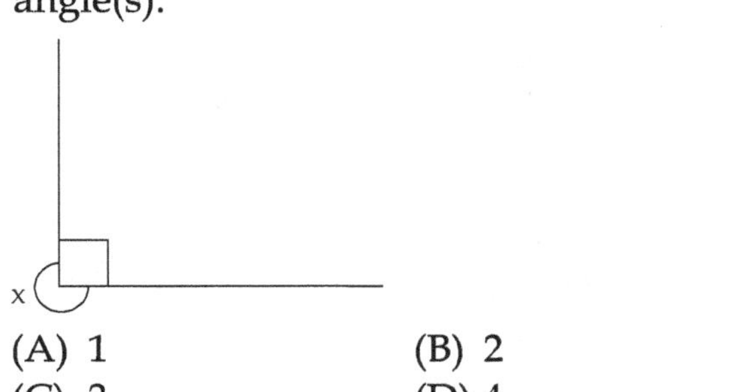

(C) (D)

27. How many right angles are there in $2\frac{1}{2}$ complete turns?

(A) 8 (B) 10
(C) 12 (D) 14

28. Angle X is equal to _________ right angle(s).

(A) 1 (B) 2
(C) 3 (D) 4

29. Count the number of triangles in the given figure.

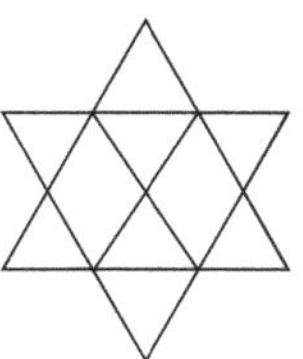

(A) 8 (B) 10
(C) 14 (D) None of these

30. Which of the following figure/net folds up to form a cube?

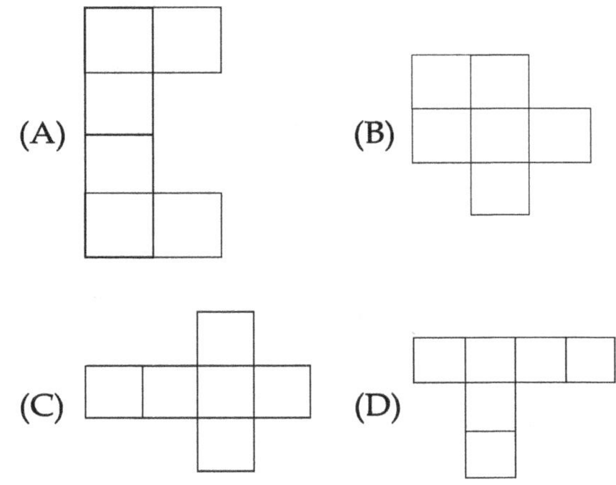

(A) (B)

(C) (D)

—Darken Your Choice with HB Pencil—

1.	Ⓐ Ⓑ Ⓒ Ⓓ	7.	Ⓐ Ⓑ Ⓒ Ⓓ	13.	Ⓐ Ⓑ Ⓒ Ⓓ	19	Ⓐ Ⓑ Ⓒ Ⓓ	25.	Ⓐ Ⓑ Ⓒ Ⓓ					
2.	Ⓐ Ⓑ Ⓒ Ⓓ	8.	Ⓐ Ⓑ Ⓒ Ⓓ	14.	Ⓐ Ⓑ Ⓒ Ⓓ	20.	Ⓐ Ⓑ Ⓒ Ⓓ	26.	Ⓐ Ⓑ Ⓒ Ⓓ					
3.	Ⓐ Ⓑ Ⓒ Ⓓ	9.	Ⓐ Ⓑ Ⓒ Ⓓ	15.	Ⓐ Ⓑ Ⓒ Ⓓ	21.	Ⓐ Ⓑ Ⓒ Ⓓ	27.	Ⓐ Ⓑ Ⓒ Ⓓ					
4.	Ⓐ Ⓑ Ⓒ Ⓓ	10.	Ⓐ Ⓑ Ⓒ Ⓓ	16.	Ⓐ Ⓑ Ⓒ Ⓓ	22.	Ⓐ Ⓑ Ⓒ Ⓓ	28.	Ⓐ Ⓑ Ⓒ Ⓓ					
5.	Ⓐ Ⓑ Ⓒ Ⓓ	11.	Ⓐ Ⓑ Ⓒ Ⓓ	17.	Ⓐ Ⓑ Ⓒ Ⓓ	23.	Ⓐ Ⓑ Ⓒ Ⓓ	29.	Ⓐ Ⓑ Ⓒ Ⓓ					
6.	Ⓐ Ⓑ Ⓒ Ⓓ	12.	Ⓐ Ⓑ Ⓒ Ⓓ	18.	Ⓐ Ⓑ Ⓒ Ⓓ	24.	Ⓐ Ⓑ Ⓒ Ⓓ	30.	Ⓐ Ⓑ Ⓒ Ⓓ					

AREA, PERIMETER AND VOLUME 

7

- ➤ Cube
- ➤ Cuboid
- ➤ Rectangle
- ➤ Cylinder
- ➤ Square
- ➤ Circle
- ➤ Cone

MULTIPLE CHOICE QUESTIONS

1. Find the area of the triangle shown.

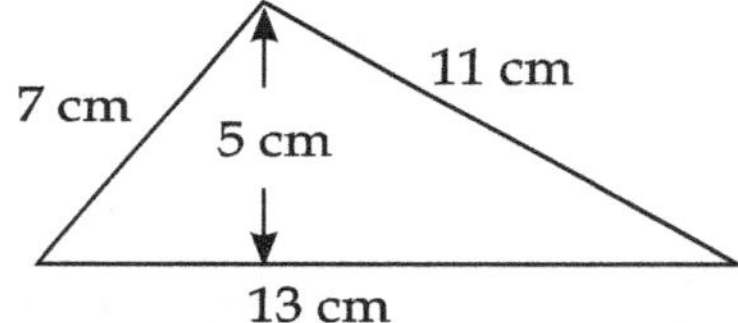

   (A) 2.5 cm²
   (B) 45.5 cm²
   (C) 65 cm²
   (D) 71.5 cm²

2. Find the perimeter of the triangle shown in the previous question.
   (A) 15.5 cm
   (B) 29 cm
   (C) 31 cm
   (D) 62 cm

3. Find the area of the parallelogram shown.

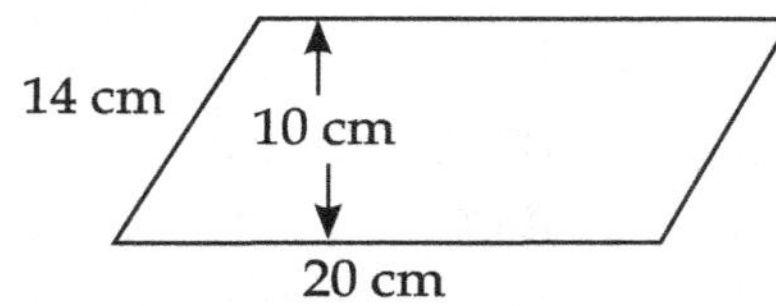

   (A) 140 cm²
   (B) 200 cm²

   (C) 240 cm²
   (D) 280 cm²

4. Find the perimeter of the parallelogram shown in the previous question.
   (A) 34 cm
   (B) 56 cm
   (C) 60 cm
   (D) 68 cm

5. Find the area of the trapezoid shown.

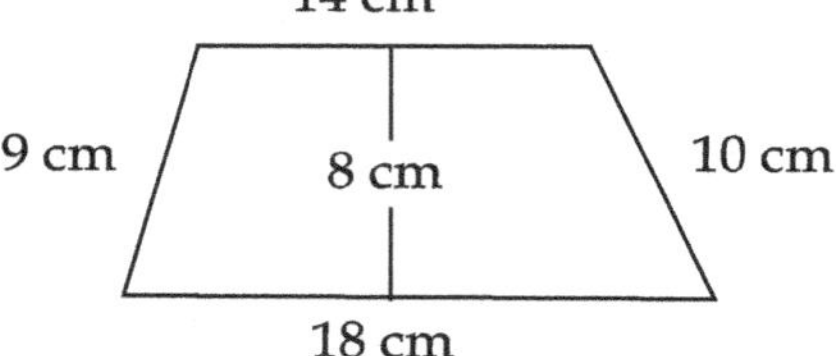

   (A) 128 cm²
   (B) 252 cm²
   (C) 256 cm²
   (D) 324 cm²

6. Find the perimeter of the trapezoid shown in the previous question.
   (A) 25.5 cm
   (B) 32 cm
   (C) 48 cm
   (D) 51 cm

7. Find the area of the circle shown.

OLYMPIAD WORKBOOK (IMO) CLASS – 5

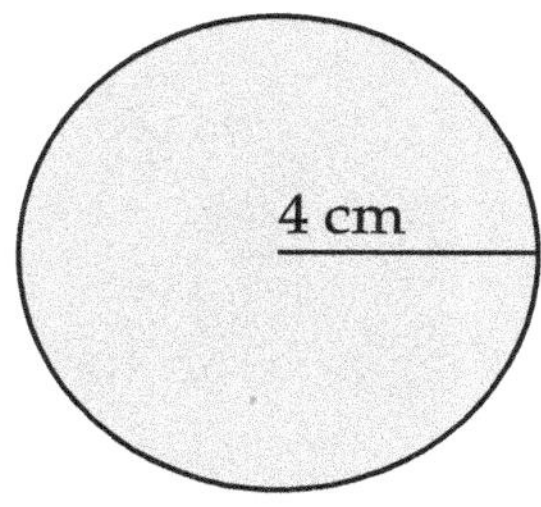

(A) 16 cm²
(B) 25 cm²
(C) 50 cm²
(D) 101 cm²

8. Find the perimeter of the circle shown in the previous question.
   (A) 12.5 cm
   (B) 25 cm
   (C) 50 cm
   (D) 101 cm

9. Find the area of the figure shown.

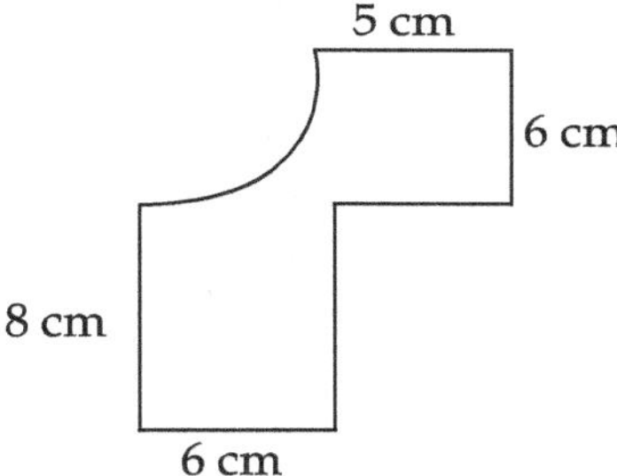

   (A) 154 cm²
   (B) 114 cm²
   (C) 85.7 cm²
   (D) 57.5 cm²

10. Find the perimeter of the figure shown in the previous question.
    (A) 47.4 cm
    (B) 56.8 cm
    (C) 75.7 cm
    (D) 94.8 cm

11. A square has an area of 64 cm². What is the length of each side?
    (A) 8 cm
    (B) 16 cm
    (C) 32 cm
    (D) 60 cm

12. The figure below is made up of 3 squares of sides 5 cm. What is the perimeter of the figure?

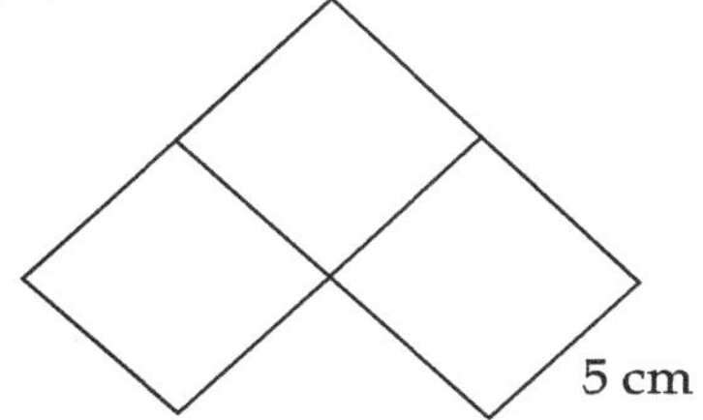

    (A) 15 cm
    (B) 30 cm
    (C) 40 cm
    (D) 50 cm

13. The figure below is made up of three squares. Find the perimeter of the figure.

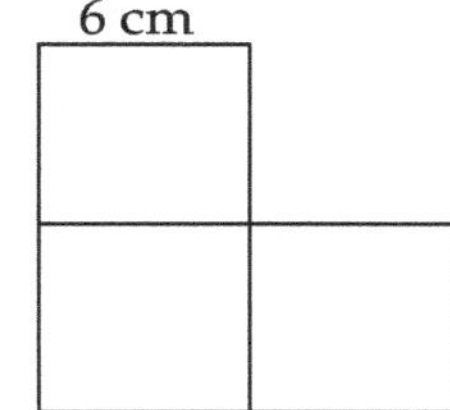

    (A) 48 cm
    (B) 60 cm
    (C) 72 cm
    (D) 144 cm

14. 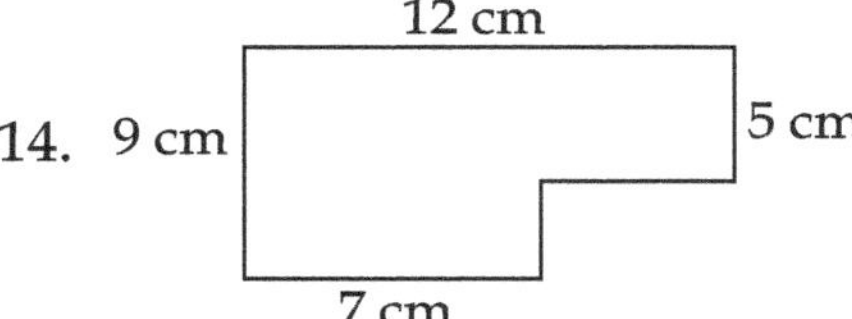

    The area of the figure above is ______ m².
    (A) 42
    (B) 88
    (C) 108
    (D) 123

15. The perimeter of a square is 20 cm. What is the length of each side of the square?
    (A) 80 cm   (B) 18 cm
    (C) 5 cm   (D) 4 cm

16. Which of the following figures have the same area?

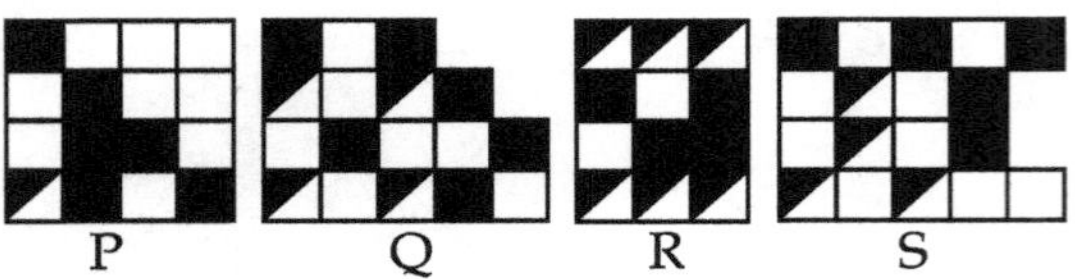

P   Q   R   S

(A) P and Q   (B) Q and R
(C) Q and S   (D) R and S

17. Which one of the following rectangles had the biggest perimeter?

(A)
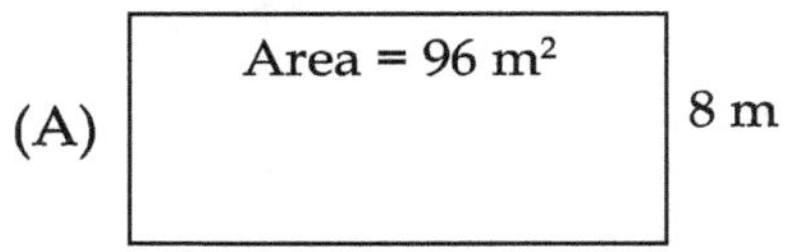
Area = 96 m²   8 m

(B)
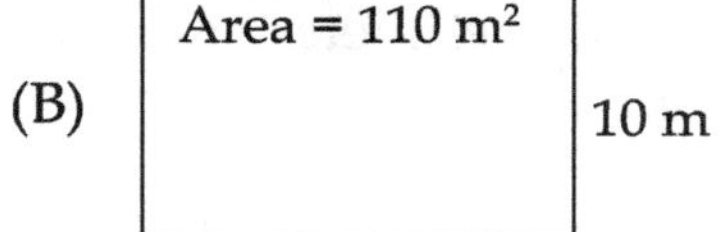
Area = 110 m²   10 m

(C)
Area = 90 m²
15 m

(D)
Area = 100 m²
25 m

18. The perimeter of the figure shown below is 36 m. What is the length of DE?

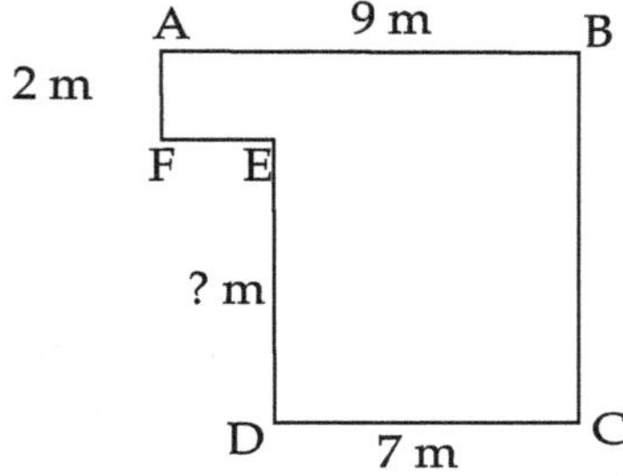

(A) 8 m
(B) 9 m
(C) 16 m
(D) 18 m

19. What is the area of the figure given below?

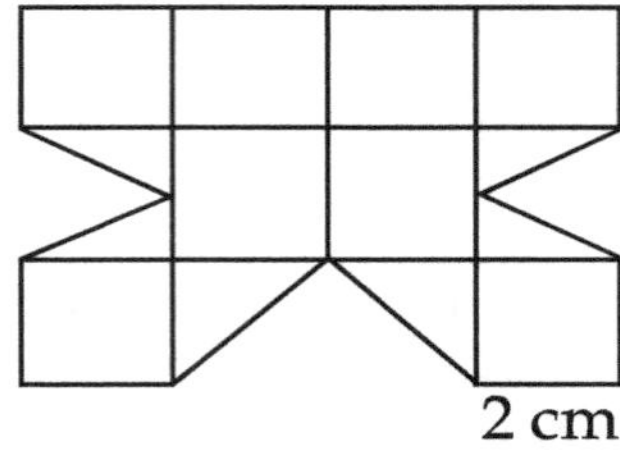

(A) 48 cm²
(B) 44 cm²
(C) 40 cm²
(D) 20 cm²

20. A rectangular garden measures 25 m by 20 m. What is the cost of erecting a wooden fence around it if every 5 metres of wooden fencing cost ₹ 27?

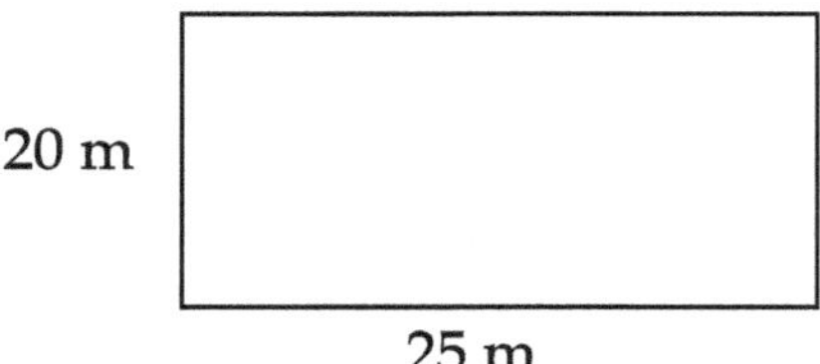

(A) ₹ 486
(B) ₹ 500
(C) ₹ 2 430
(D) ₹ 2 700

21. How many small cubes of side 2 cm can be put in a cubical box of side 6 cm?

    (A) 9 (B) 12

    (C) 27 (D) 611

22. A cuboid measures 24 m × 12 m × 16 m. How many cubes of side 8 m can fit in the box?

    (A) 9 (B) 16

    (C) 15 (D) 24

23. Find area of unshaded region if each box = 3 m².

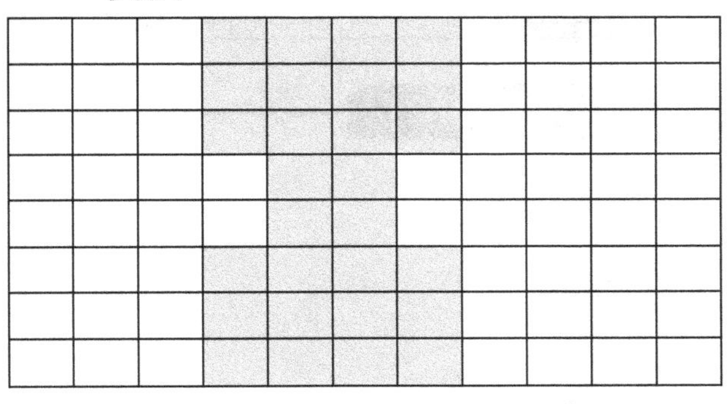

    (A) 88 m² (B) 60 m²

    (C) 84 m² (D) 180 m²

24. Identify the correct shape by seeing the following features:

    A. It's length and breadth are equal.

    B. Its area is side × side.

    C. Its perimeter is 4 times its side.

    D. It is a four-sided polygon.

    (A) Rectangle

    (B) Parallelogram

    (C) Square

    (D) Trapezium

25. How many of the following letters have only 2 lines of symmetry?

    (A) 0

    (B) 1

    (C) 2

    (D) 3

Darken Your Choice with HB Pencil

1.	Ⓐ Ⓑ Ⓒ Ⓓ	6.	Ⓐ Ⓑ Ⓒ Ⓓ	11.	Ⓐ Ⓑ Ⓒ Ⓓ	16	Ⓐ Ⓑ Ⓒ Ⓓ	21.	Ⓐ Ⓑ Ⓒ Ⓓ
2.	Ⓐ Ⓑ Ⓒ Ⓓ	7.	Ⓐ Ⓑ Ⓒ Ⓓ	12.	Ⓐ Ⓑ Ⓒ Ⓓ	17.	Ⓐ Ⓑ Ⓒ Ⓓ	22.	Ⓐ Ⓑ Ⓒ Ⓓ
3.	Ⓐ Ⓑ Ⓒ Ⓓ	8.	Ⓐ Ⓑ Ⓒ Ⓓ	13.	Ⓐ Ⓑ Ⓒ Ⓓ	18.	Ⓐ Ⓑ Ⓒ Ⓓ	23.	Ⓐ Ⓑ Ⓒ Ⓓ
4.	Ⓐ Ⓑ Ⓒ Ⓓ	9.	Ⓐ Ⓑ Ⓒ Ⓓ	14.	Ⓐ Ⓑ Ⓒ Ⓓ	19.	Ⓐ Ⓑ Ⓒ Ⓓ	24.	Ⓐ Ⓑ Ⓒ Ⓓ
5.	Ⓐ Ⓑ Ⓒ Ⓓ	10.	Ⓐ Ⓑ Ⓒ Ⓓ	15.	Ⓐ Ⓑ Ⓒ Ⓓ	20.	Ⓐ Ⓑ Ⓒ Ⓓ	25.	Ⓐ Ⓑ Ⓒ Ⓓ

SYMMETRY

LEARNING OBJECTIVES

➤ Line of Symmetry
➤ Rotational Symmetry

MULTIPLE CHOICE QUESTIONS

State the order of rotational symmetry from question 1 to 7

1.

(A) 3   (B) 4
(C) 5   (D) 7

2. 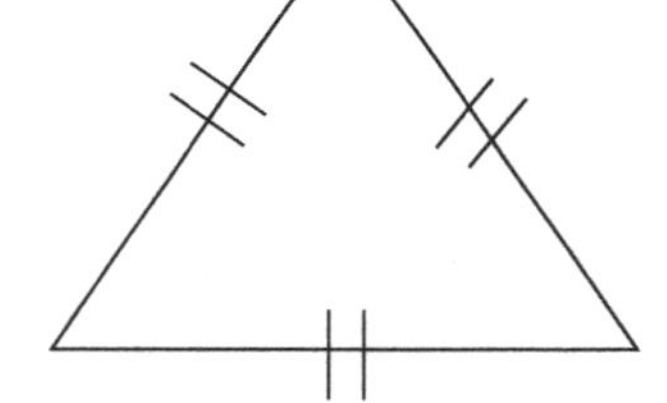

(A) 1   (B) 2
(C) 3   (D) 4

3. 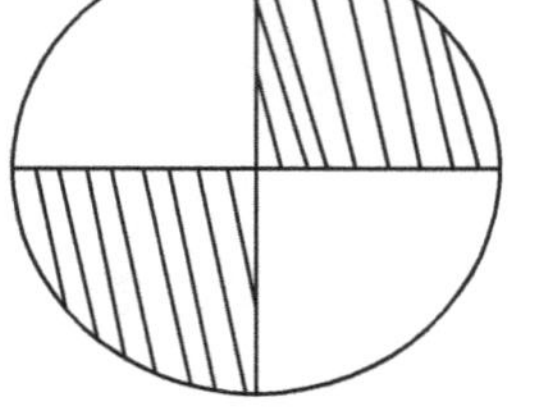

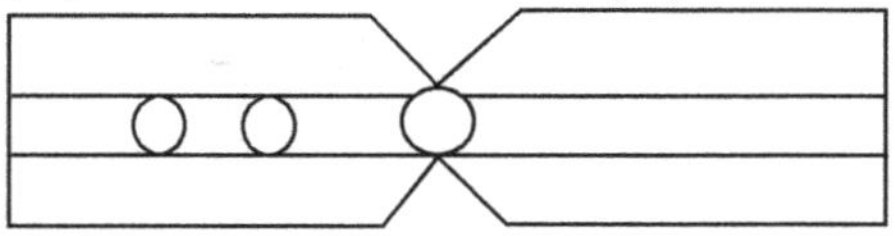

(A) 1   (B) 2
(C) 3   (D) 6

4.

(A) 3   (B) 4
(C) 5   (D) 2

5. 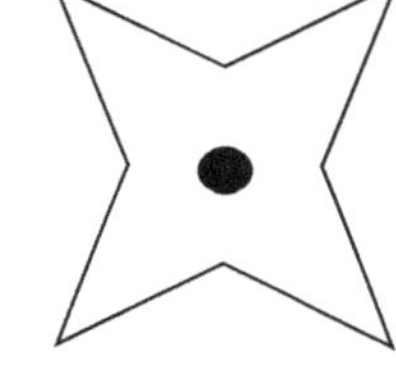

(A) 1   (B) 2
(C) 3   (D) 5

6. 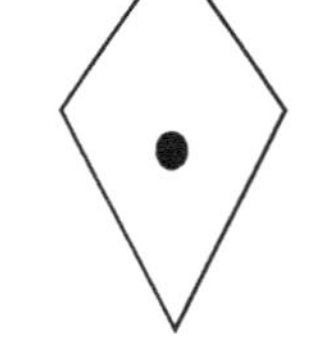

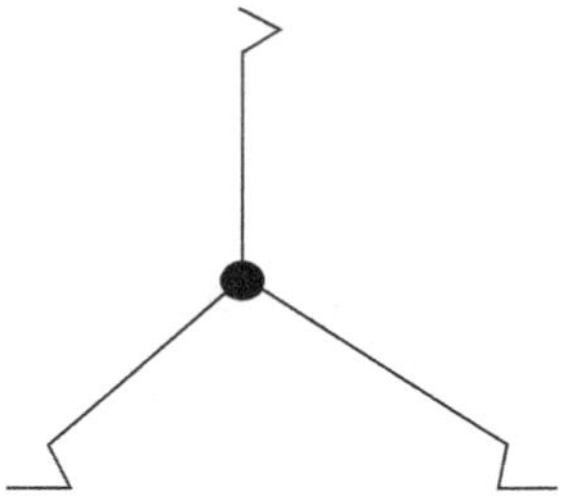

(A) 1   (B) 2
(C) 3   (D) 7

OLYMPIAD WORKBOOK (IMO) CLASS – 5

7.

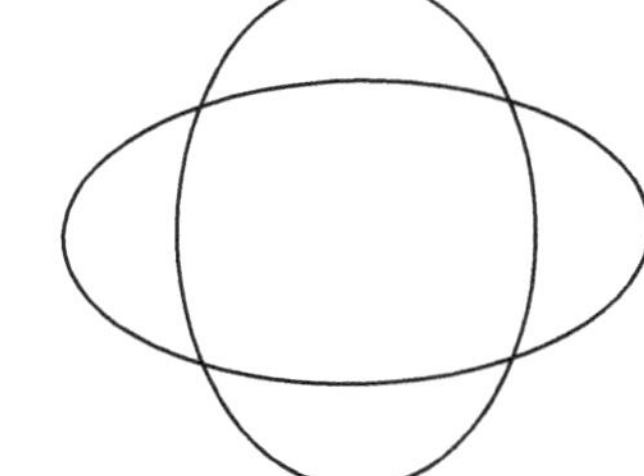

(A) 5   (B) 4
(C) 3   (D) 2

8. An object is said to be symmetrical if __________
   (A) It can divide into two or more identical pieces
   (B) It can divide into multiple pieces
   (C) It cannot divide
   (D) none of the above

9. Line of symmetry is__________
   (A) The line that divides a figure into non identical pieces
   (B) The line that divides a figure into two or more identical pieces
   (C) The line that passes through the centre of the figure
   (D) none of the above

10. Draw its line of symmetry.

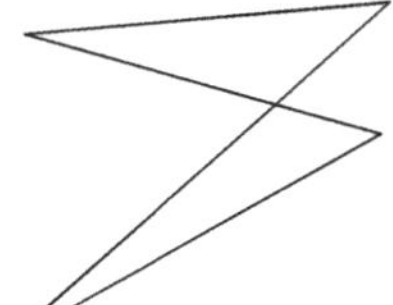

(A) No line of symmetry

(B) 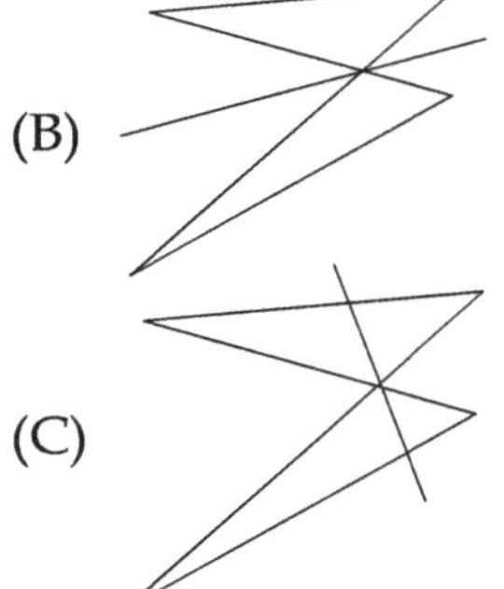

(C)

(D) 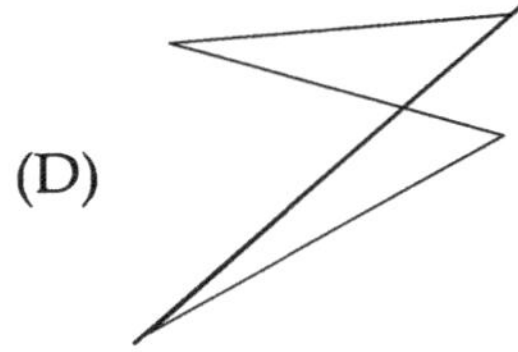

11. Choose the figure that is symmetric.

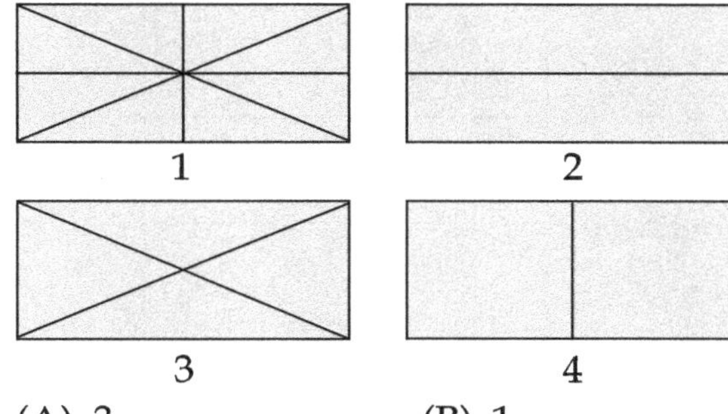

(A) 3   (B) 1
(C) Both 2 and 4   (D) 2

12. Draw the lines of symmetry.

(A)   (B)

(C) 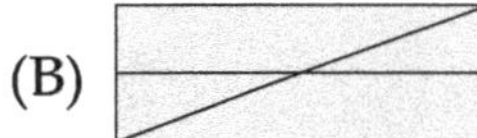   (D)

13. Which of the following dotted lines is the line of symmetry for the given figure?

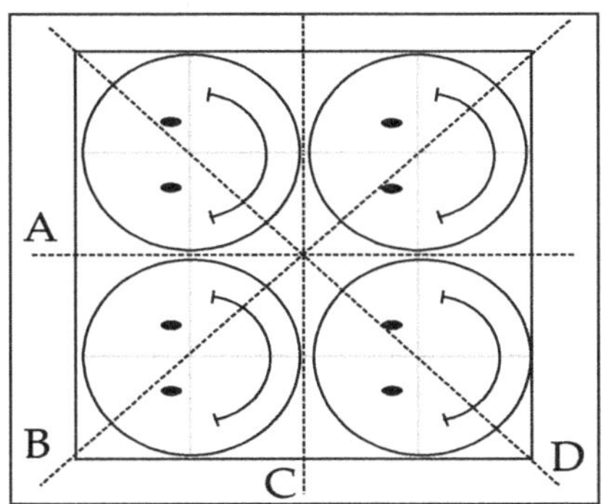

(A) A   (B) B
(C) C   (D) D

14. How many more lines of symmetry does Figure (II) have than Figure (I)?

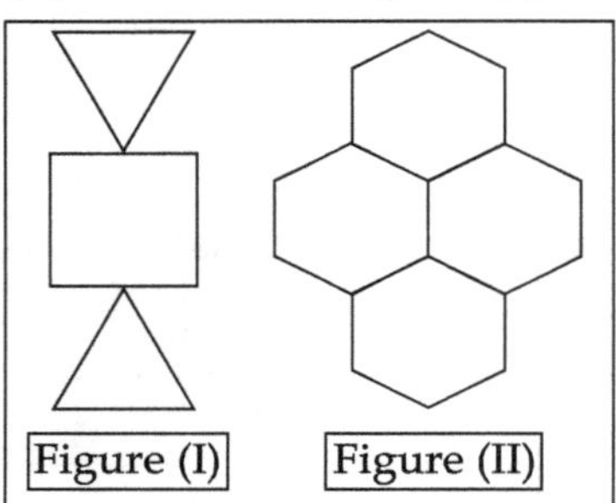

(A) 0   (B) 1
(C) 2   (D) 3

15. What is the least number of squares that must be added so that the line PQ becomes a line of symmetry?

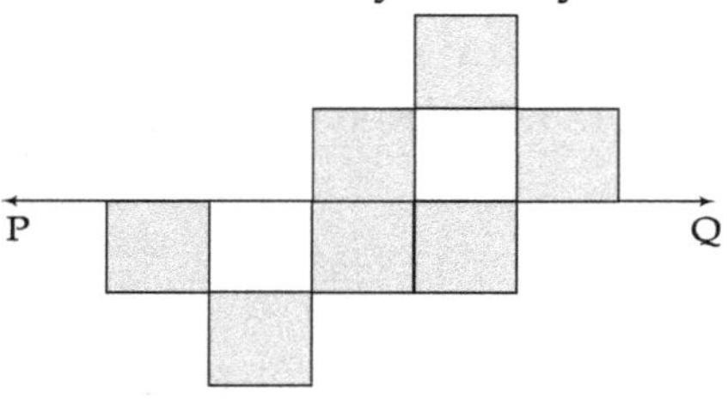

(A) 4   (B) 5
(C) 6   (D) 9

16. What is the rotational symmetry of a figure when the object is placed at one of the vertices of an equilateral triangle?

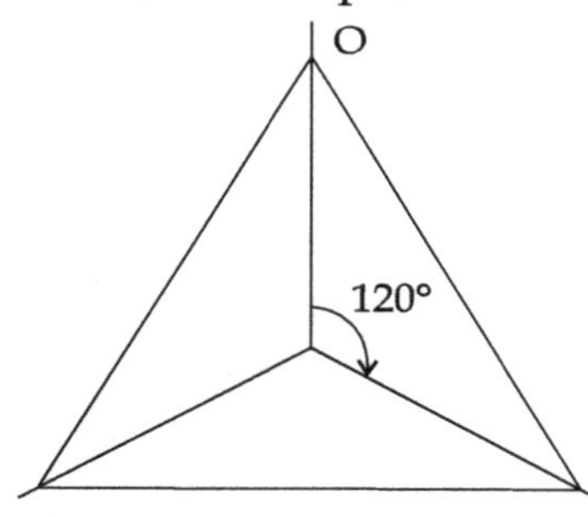

(A 0   (B) 1
(C) 2   (D) 3

17. How many more squares in the figure must be drawn so that the figure becomes symmetrical along the dotted line?

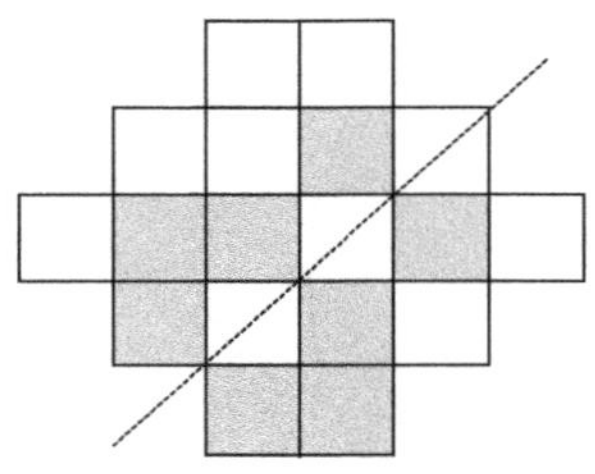

(A) 1   (B) 3
(C) 6   (D) 8

18. Which of the following is a line of symmetry of the figure?

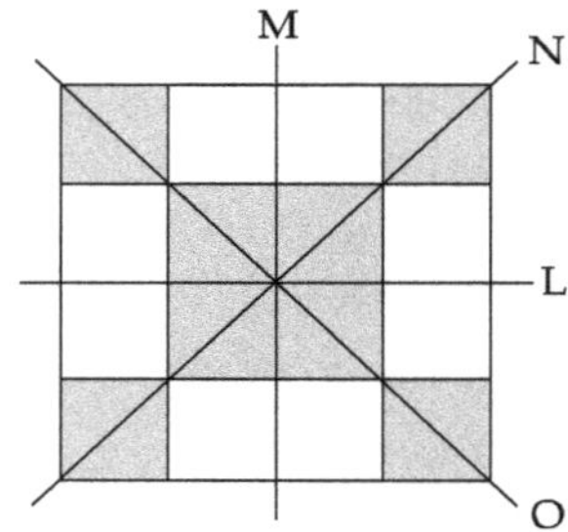

(A) Both L and O
(B) Both L and N
(C) Only N
(D) AII L, M, N and O

19. What is the least number of squares that must be added, so that the line AB becomes a line of symmetry?

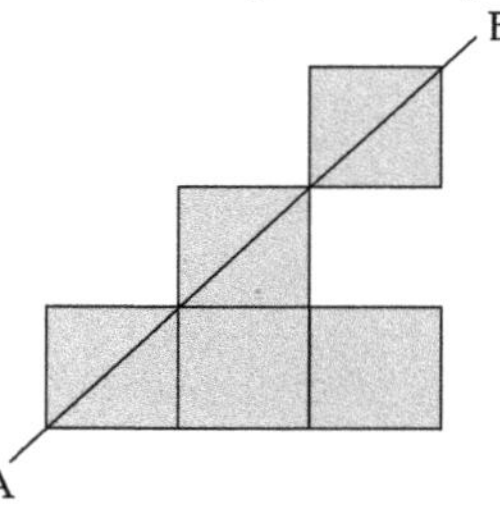

(A) 1   (B) 2
(C) 3   (D) 2

20. How many of the following letters have atleast one line of symmetry?

SINGAPORE

(A) 5   (B) 4
(C) 3   (D) 2

21. Which square must be shaded so that the figure has a line of symmetry?

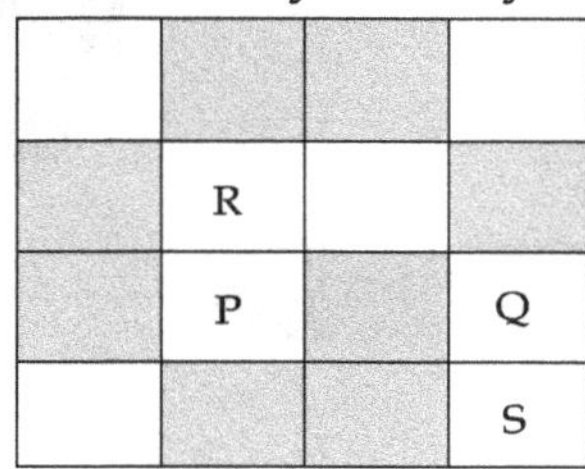

(A) P
(B) Q
(C) R
(D) S

22. What is the smallest number of squares that must be shaded so that the figure has a line of symmetry?

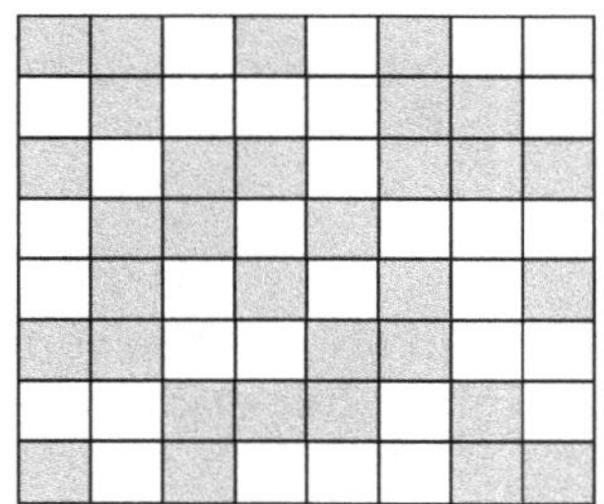

(A) 1
(B) 3
(C) 5
(D) 7

23. What is the smallest number of squares that must be added so that the line AB becomes a line of symmetry?

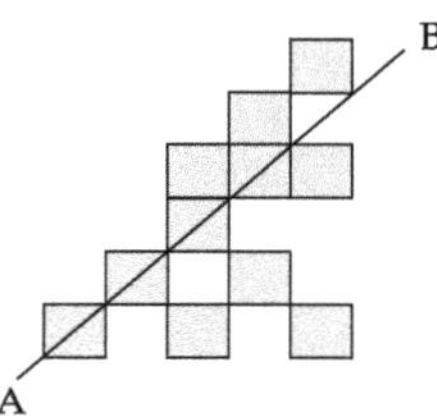

(A) 1
(C) 5
(B) 2
(D) 4

24. How many Lines of symmetry does the figure have?

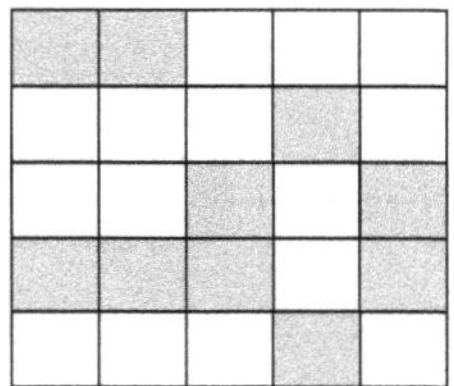

(A) 0
(C) 2
(B) 1
(D) 4

25. The minimum number of squares that must be shaded, so that the figure has a line of symmetry is __________.

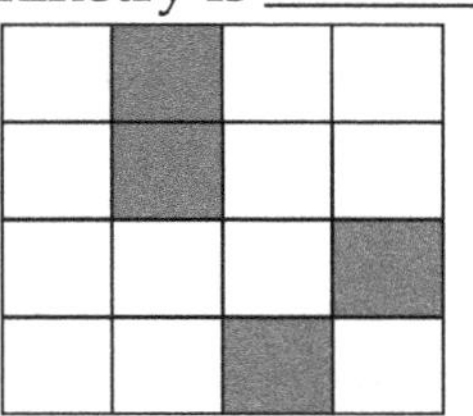

(A) 1
(C) 3
(B) 2
(D) 0

DATA HANDLING

LEARNING OBJECTIVES

➤ Qualitative and Quantitative Data
➤ Census or Sample

MULTIPLE CHOICE QUESTIONS

1. The bar graph shows the results when a die was thrown a number of times.

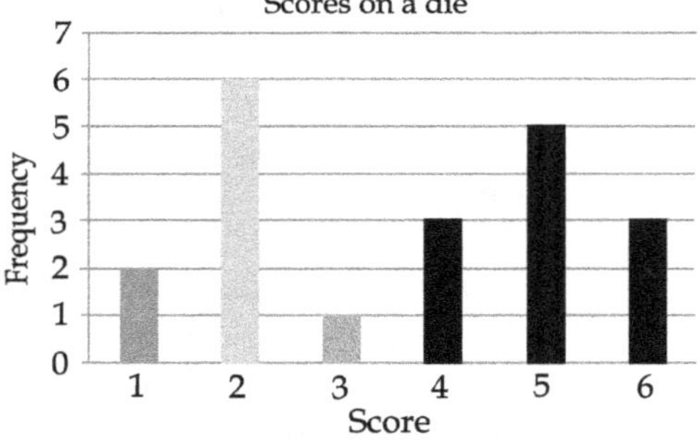

   How many sixes were thrown?
   (A) 2
   (B) 3
   (C) 5
   (D) 6

2. The bar graph shows the favourite colors of 20 students in a class.

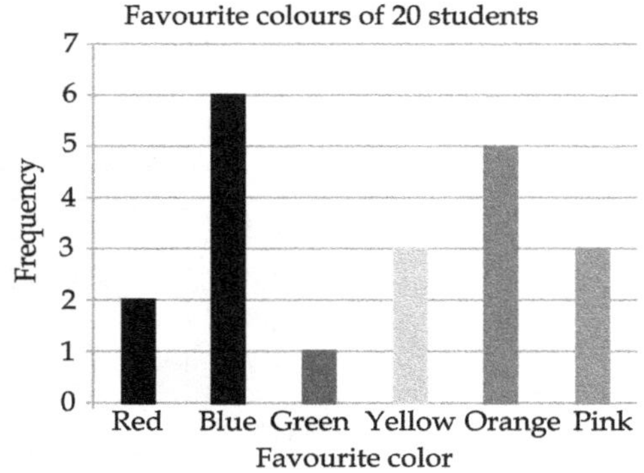

How many more of them favoured orange than those who favoured green?
(A) 2
(B) 3
(C) 4
(D) 5

3. The bar graph shows the scores obtained by Shraddha in her end of year exams.

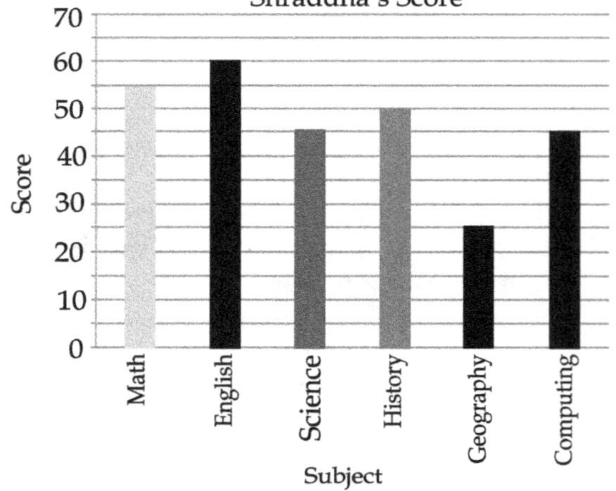

How much more did Shraddha score in her best subject than in her worst subject?
(A) 25
(B) 35
(C) 45
(D) 60

4. The bar graph shows the scores obtained by Shraddha in her end of year exams.

OLYMPIAD WORKBOOK (IMO) CLASS– 5

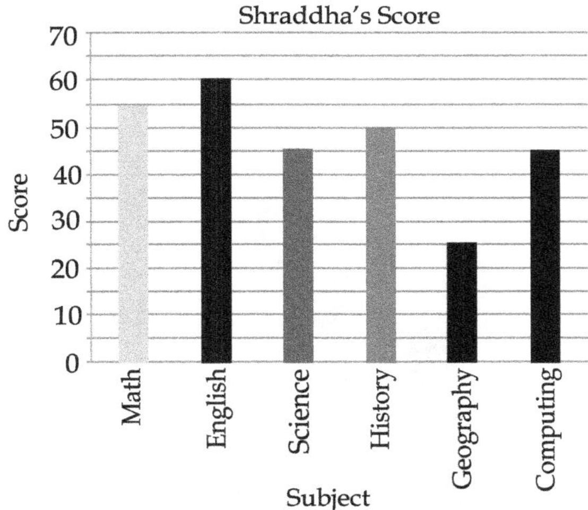

Shubhra's score in English was 15% higher than Shraddha's score in English. What was Shubhra's score in English?

(A) 89   (B) 79
(C) 72   (D) 69

5. The pie chart shows the amount of time that Shraddha spends on various activities each day.

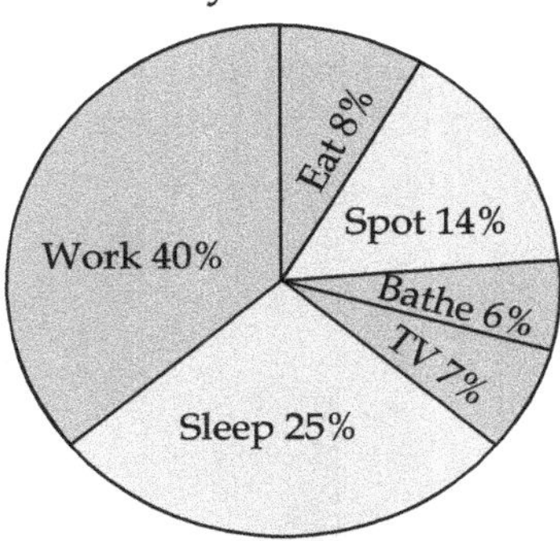

If this information were displayed using a bar graph with hours on the vertical axis, what would be the height of the bar for sleep?

(A) 8 hours   (B) 7 hours
(C) 6 hours   (D) 2.5 hours

6. Shraddha recorded the amount of time she spent on six activities over a twenty four hour period and drew a bar graph, as follows:

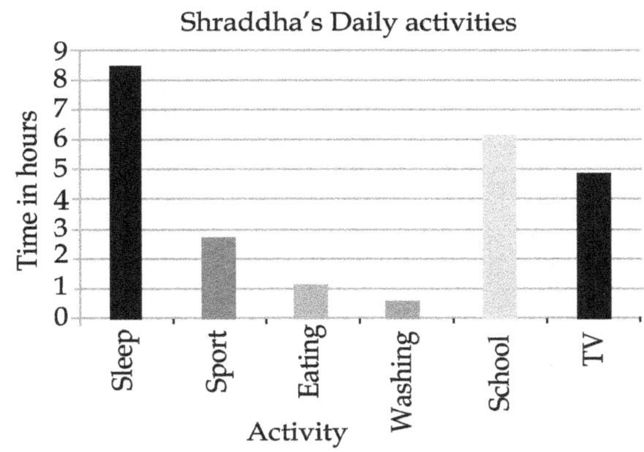

Approximately how many more hours did she spend sleeping than watching TV?

(A) About 3½ hours longer
(B) About 4 hours longer
(C) About 4½ hours longer
(D) About 5 hours longer

7. Shraddha recorded the temperature in her room (in Degrees Fahrenheit) every two hours over a 12 hour period from noon to midnight. The results are shown in the line graph.

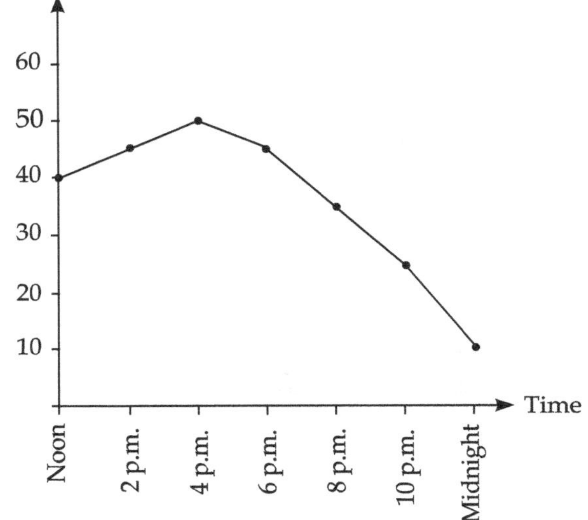

What was the approximate temperature in her room at 9 p.m.?

(A) 35°F   (B) 30°F
(C) 25°F   (D) 20°F

8. The line graph shows how the record time for the 100 m sprint changed from 1964 when Bob Hayes of the US held the record to 2012 when Usain Bolt of Jamaica held the record.

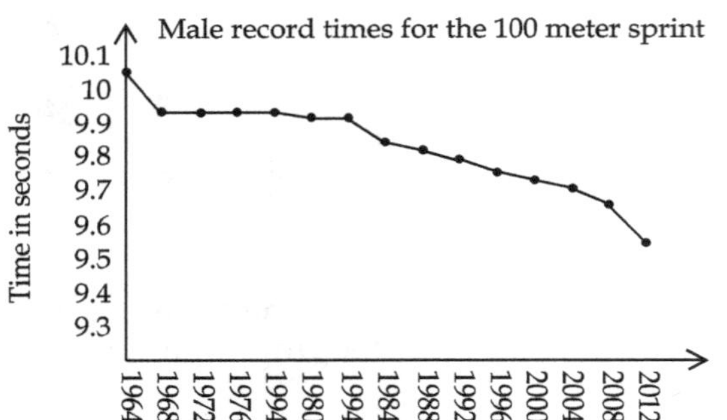

From the graph, what was the maximum length of time for which the record remained unchanged?

(A) 3 years
(B) 9 years
(C) 12 years
(D) 16 years

9. The histogram shows the heights of 21 students in a class, grouped into 5-inch groups.

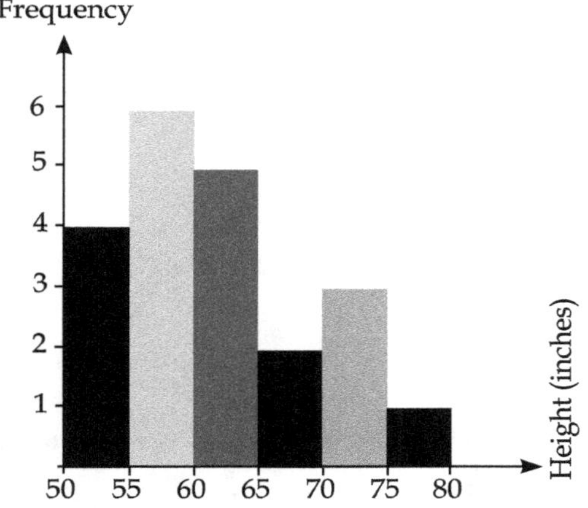

How many students were greater than or equal to 60 inches tall?

(A) 21
(B) 17
(C) 11
(D) 6

10. The histogram shows the heights of 21 students in a class, grouped into 5 inches groups.

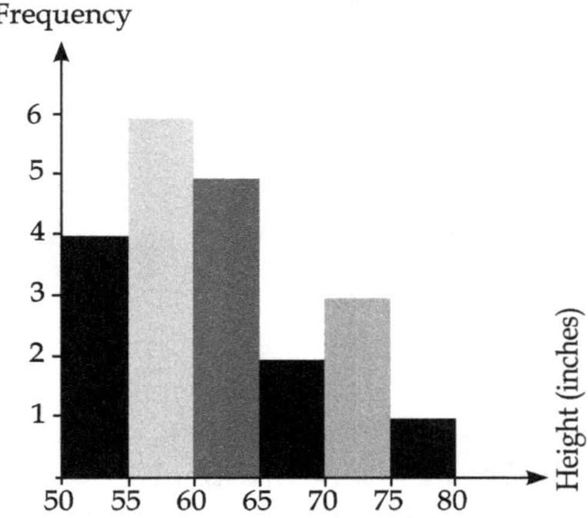

How many students were greater than or equal to 55 inches tall but less than 70 inches tall?

(A) 13
(B) 15
(C) 16
(D) 17

11. A class carried out an experiment to measure the lengths of cuckoo eggs. The length of each egg was measured to the nearest mm. The results are shown in the following histogram:

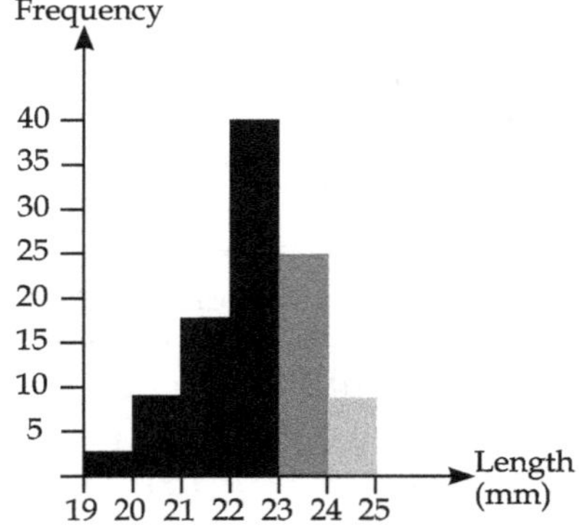

How many eggs were measured altogether in the experiment?

(A) 25
(B) 40
(C) 90
(D) 100

OLYMPIAD WORKBOOK (IMO) CLASS– 5

12. The histogram shows the birth weights of 100 new born babies. Babies who weigh less than 5 lb are considered to have a low birth weight. Babies who weigh 10 lb or more are considered to have a high birth weight.

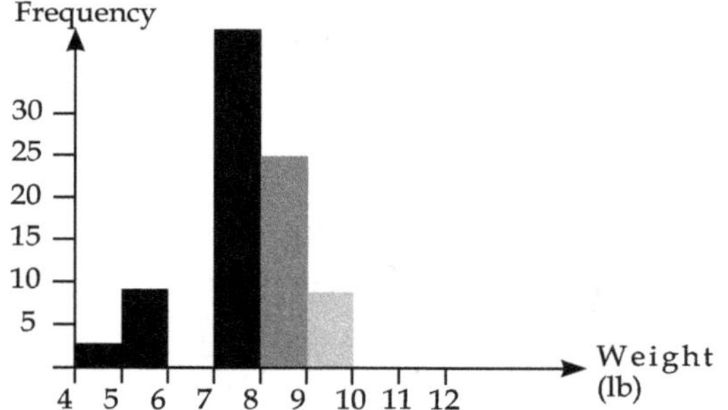

What percent of the babies had neither a low nor a high birth weight?

(A) 97% (B) 91%
(C) 85% (D) 83%

13. Which letter occurs the most frequently in the following sentence?

THE SUN ALWAYS SETS IN THE WEST.

(A) E (B) S
(C) T (D) W

14. A fair die was thrown 100 times. The frequency distribution is shown in the following table:

Score	Frequency
1	16
2	18
3	11
4	15
5	19
6	21

How many throws scored less than 3?

(A) 11 (B) 34
(C) 45 (D) 56

15. 60 students sat for a test. The frequency distribution is shown in the following table:

Mark	Frequency
0	1
1	3
2	6
3	9
4	8
5	11
6	8
7	7
8	4
9	1
10	2

How many students scored 5 or more?

(A) 11 (B) 22
(C) 33 (D) 38

16. 60 students sat for a test. The frequency distribution is shown in the following table:

Mark	Frequency
0	1
1	3
2	6
3	9
4	8
5	11
6	8
7	7
8	4
9	1
10	2

How many students scored greater than or equal to 4, but less than or equal to 7?

(A) 19 (B) 26
(C) 27 (D) 34

17. Shraddha did a survey of the number of pets owned by her classmates, with the following results:

Number of pets	Frequency
0	4
1	12
2	8
3	2
4	1
5	2
6	1

How many of her classmates had less than 3 pets?

(A) 16   (B) 20

(C) 24   (D) 26

18. The children in a class did a survey of the number of siblings (brothers and sisters) each of them had. The results are recorded in the following table:

Number of siblings	Frequency
0	3
1	6
2	8
3	5
4	4
5	2
6	1
7	0
8	0
9	1

How many families had more than 4 children?

(A) 4

(B) 5

(C) 8

(D) 13

19. Which one of the following is discrete data?

(A) Sam is 160 cm tall

(B) Sam has two brothers and one sister

(C) Sam weighs 60 kg

(D) Sam ran 100 meters in 10.2 seconds

20. Lisa conducted a survey of the cars passing her house. How many cars passed in total?

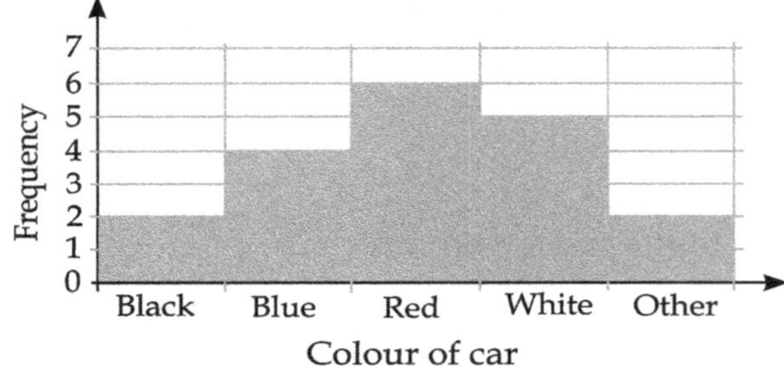

(A) 17

(B) 19

(C) 23

(D) 40

HOTS (ACHIEVERS SECTION)

Following pie chart shows the percentage of males and females in a city with population over 1,00,000.

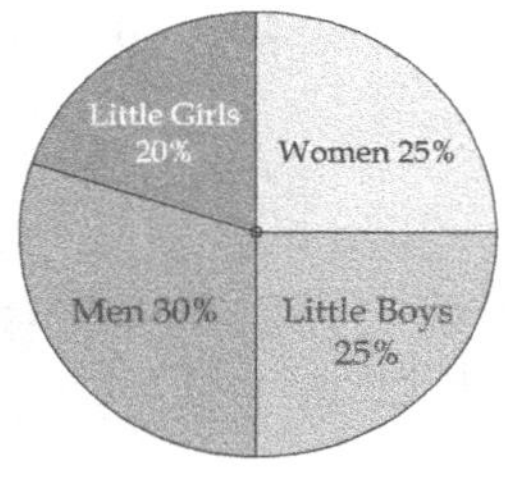

21. What is the sum of the numbers of little girls and women in the city?

(a) 44,000

(b) 45,000

(c) 45,500

(d) 42,100

22. Following bar graph represents the number of present students in class 5th in a particular week.

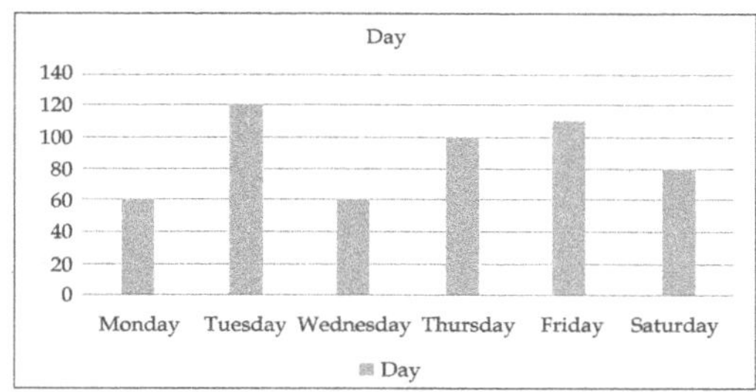

If there are 150 students in the class 5th, how many students were absent on Friday?

(a) 20   (b) 80

(c) 30   (d) 40

23. The column graph shows the number of books (in thousands) sold by a shop owner during the first 6 months of a certain year.

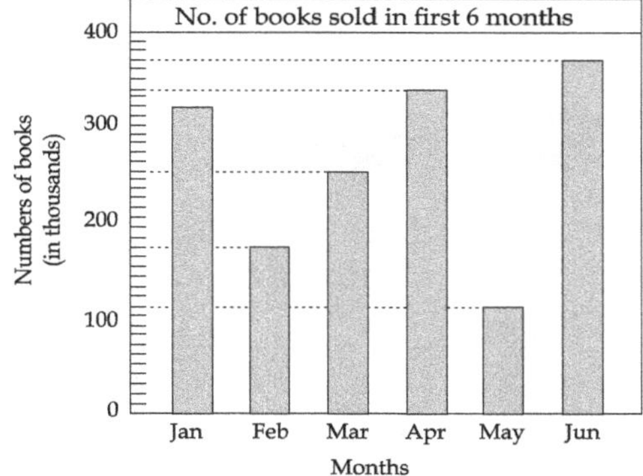

In which month is the number of books sold twice as many as those sold in February?

(a) February   (b) May

(c) April   (d) January

24. The incomplete pictograph shows the amount of money Dinesh spent on four days.

Day	Money spent
Monday	◯ ◯ ◯ ◯
Tuesday	◯ ◯
Wednesday	◯ ◯ ◯
Thursday	◯ ◯ ◯ ◯ ◯
Friday	◯
Saturday	◯ ◯ ◯ ◯
Sunday	

Each ◯ stands for ₹ 50

If Golu spent ₹ 500 in weekend (Saturday and Sunday), how many symbols must be drawn for Sunday?

(a) 5   (b) 6

(c) 9   (d) 10

25. The table shows how rabbits grew every year. After which year did the number of rabbits cross 1000?

Times	Numbers of rabbits
Start	10
1 year	18
2 year	32
3 year	58
4 year	105
5 year	
6 year	

(a) 5 years   (b) 6 years

(c) 8 years   (d) 10 years

LOGICAL REASONING

LEARNING OBJECTIVES

- ➤ Completion of series
- ➤ Relationship between words
- ➤ Odd word
- ➤ Letter Coding
- ➤ Alphabetical Order of Words
- ➤ Directions and Cardinal directions
- ➤ Water Images of Capital Letters
- ➤ Figure Pattern
- ➤ Relationship between events
- ➤ Number alphabet
- ➤ Number to Letter Coding
- ➤ Letter-Word Problems
- ➤ Mirror Images of Capital Letters

MULTIPLE CHOICE QUESTIONS

1. Find the missing element:
   2Z5, 7Y7, 14X9, 23W11, 34V13, ?
   (A) 27U24   (B) 47U15
   (C) 45U15   (D) 47V14

2. Find the missing element:
   P3C, R5F, T8I, V12L, ?
   (A) Y17O   (B) X17M
   (C) X17O   (D) X16O

3. Find the missing element:
   J2Z, K4X, 17V, ?, H16R, M22P
   (A) L11S   (B) L12T
   (C) L11T   (D) L12S

4. Find the missing element:
   3F, 6G, 11I, 18L, ?
   (A) 21O   (B) 25N
   (C) 27P   (D) 27Q

5. Find the missing element:
   D-4, F-6, H-8, J-10, ?, ?
   (A) K-12, M-13   (B) L-12, M-14
   (C) L-12, N-14   (D) K-12, M-14

6. Anthropology is related to Man in the same way as Anthology is related to
   (A) Nature   (B) Trees
   (C) Apes   (D) Poems

7. What is related to Leaves in the same way as Chatter is related to Teeth?
   (A) Whistle   (B) Ripple
   (C) Rustle   (D) Cackle

8. Lion is related to Prowl in the same way as Bear is related to?
   (A) Frisk   (B) Lumber
   (C) Stride   (D) Bound

9. Mirror is related to Reflection in the same way as Water is related to
   (A) Conduction   (B) Dispersion
   (C) Immersion   (D) Refraction

10. Firm is related to Flabby in the same way as Piquant is related to
    (A) Bland   (B) Salty
    (C) Pleasant   (D) Small

11. (A) Manganese   (B) Rubber
     (C) Salt   (D) Gold

12. (A) Rectangle   (B) Rhombus
     (C) Square   (D) Circle

13. (A) Bark   (B) Cry
     (C) Chirp   (D) Roar

14. (A) Aluminium   (B) Copper
     (C) Brass   (D) Brick

15. (A) Metre   (B) Yard
     (C) Litre   (D) Inch

16. If GIVE is coded as 5137 and BAT is coded as 924, how is GATE coded?
    (A) 5427
    (B) 2547
    (C) 5247
    (D) 5724

17. If in a certain code, LUTE is written as MUTE and FATE is written as GATE, then how will BLUE be written in that code?
    (A) CLUE
    (B) GLUE
    (C) FLUE
    (D) SLUE

18. In a certain code, INSTITUTION is written as NOITUTITSNI. How is PERFECTION written in that code?
    (A) NOICTEFREP
    (B) NOITCEFERP
    (C) NOITCEFREP
    (D) NOITCEFPER

19. In a certain code, GIGANTIC is written as GIGTANCI. How is MIRACLES written in that code?
    (A) MIRLCAES
    (B) MIRLACSE
    (C) RIMCALSE
    (D) RIMLCAES

20. In a certain code, GOODNESS is written as HNPCODTR. How is GREATNESS written in that code?
    (A) HQFZUODTR
    (B) HQFZUMFRT
    (C) HQFZSMFRT
    (D) FSDBSODTR

21. How many pairs of letters in the word 'CATASTROPHE' have as many letters between them in the word as in the alphabet?
    (A) One
    (B) Two
    (C) Three
    (D) Four
    (E) None of these

22. How many pairs of letters are there in the word 'SEQUENTIAL' which have as many letters between them as in the alphabet?
    (A) Nil
    (B) One
    (C) Two
    (D) Three
    (E) Four

23. How many pairs of letters are there in the word 'REPURCUSSION' which have as many letters between them in the word as in the alphabet and that too in the same order? (Do not consider the pairs 'US' and 'ON'.)
    (A) Nil
    (B) One
    (C) Two
    (D) Three
    (E) None of these

24. How many pairs of letters are there in the word 'PRESENTMENT' which have as many letters between them in the word as in the alphabet?
    (A) Nil
    (B) One
    (C) Two
    (D) Three
    (E) None of these

25. How many pairs of letters are there in the word 'ADEQUATELY' which have as many letters between them in the word as in the alphabet?
(A) One
(B) Two
(C) Three
(D) Four
(E) More than four

26. Golu starts from his house towards West. After walking a distance of 30 metres, he turned towards right and walked 20 metres. He then turned left and moving a distance of 10 metres, turned to his left again and walked 40 metres. He now turns to the left and walks 5 metres. Finally he turns to his left. In which direction is he walking now?
(A) North
(B) South
(C) East
(D) South-west

27. A rat runs towards East and turns to right, runs and turns to right, runs and again turns to left, runs and then turns to left, runs and finally turns to left and runs. Now, which direction is the rat facing?
(A) East
(B) West
(C) North
(D) South

28. Suraj walks 10 metres towards the South. Turning to the left, he walks 20 metres and then moves to his right. After moving a distance of 20 metres, he turns to the right and walks 20 metres. Finally, he turns to the right and moves a distance of 10 metres. How far and in which direction is he from the starting point?
(A) 10 metres North
(B) 20 metres South
(C) 20 metres North
(D) 10 metres South

29. I am facing South. I turn right and walk 20 m. Then I turn right again and walk 10 m. Then I turn left and walk 10 m and then turning right walk 20 m. Then I turn right again and walk 60 m. In which direction am I from the starting point?
(A) North
(B) North-West
(C) East
(D) North-East

30. Anil went 15 kms to the West from my house, then turned left and walked 20 kms. He then turned East and walked 25 kms and finally turning left covered 20 kms. How far was he from his house?
(A) 5 kms
(B) 10 kms
(C) 40 kms
(D) 80 kms

31. Choose the correct mirror image of the given figure (X) from amongst the four alternatives.

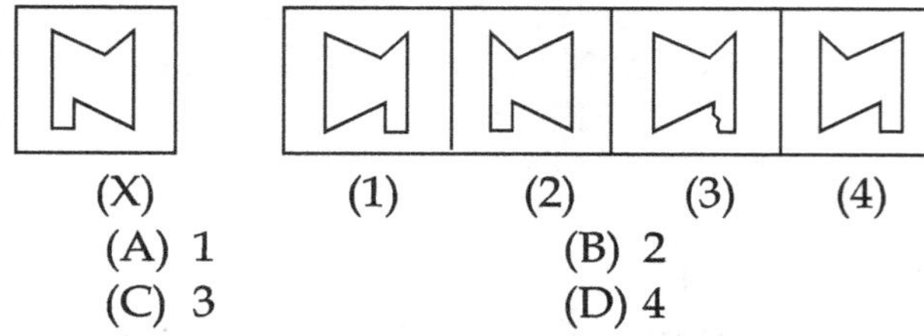

(X)   (1)   (2)   (3)   (4)
(A) 1   (B) 2
(C) 3   (D) 4

32. Choose the correct mirror image of the given figure (X) from amongst the four alternatives.

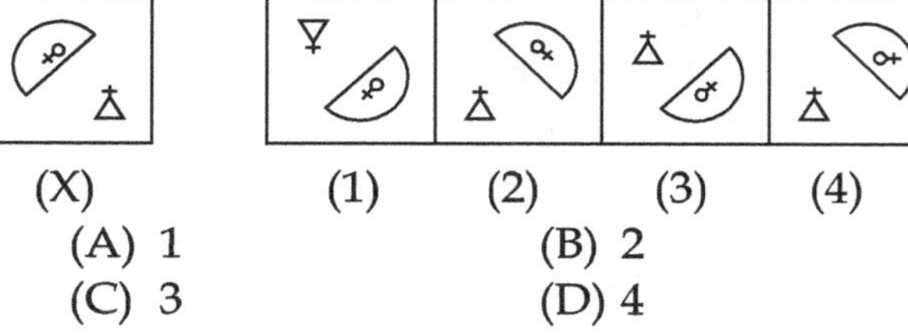

(X)   (1)   (2)   (3)   (4)
(A) 1   (B) 2
(C) 3   (D) 4

33. Choose the correct mirror image of the given figure (X) from amongst the four alternatives.

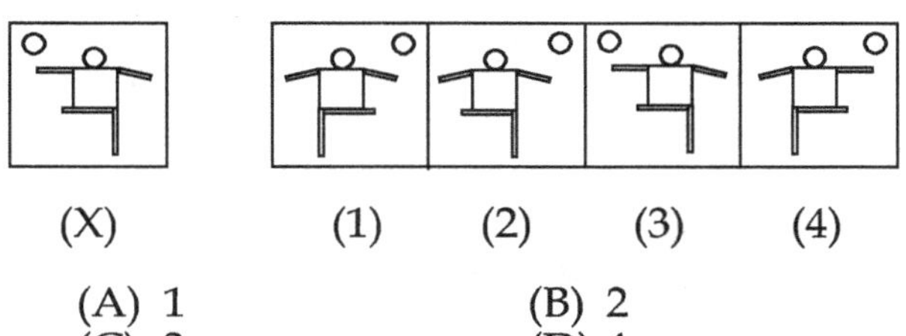

   (X)   (1)   (2)   (3)   (4)

   (A) 1   (B) 2
   (C) 3   (D) 4

Directions: In the following questions, a word is followed by four alternatives, (A) (B), (C) and (D) showing possible water images of that word. Choose the alternative which shows the correct water image of that word.

34. CLOSELY
   (A) CLOSELY
   (B) CLOSELY
   (C) CLOSELY
   (D) CLOSELY

35. IMAGES
   (A) IMAGES
   (B) SEGAMI
   (C) IMAGES
   (D) IMAGES

1.	Ⓐ Ⓑ Ⓒ Ⓓ	8.	Ⓐ Ⓑ Ⓒ Ⓓ	15.	Ⓐ Ⓑ Ⓒ Ⓓ	22	Ⓐ Ⓑ Ⓒ Ⓓ	29.	Ⓐ Ⓑ Ⓒ Ⓓ
2.	Ⓐ Ⓑ Ⓒ Ⓓ	9.	Ⓐ Ⓑ Ⓒ Ⓓ	16.	Ⓐ Ⓑ Ⓒ Ⓓ	23.	Ⓐ Ⓑ Ⓒ Ⓓ	30.	Ⓐ Ⓑ Ⓒ Ⓓ
3.	Ⓐ Ⓑ Ⓒ Ⓓ	10.	Ⓐ Ⓑ Ⓒ Ⓓ	17.	Ⓐ Ⓑ Ⓒ Ⓓ	24.	Ⓐ Ⓑ Ⓒ Ⓓ	31.	Ⓐ Ⓑ Ⓒ Ⓓ
4.	Ⓐ Ⓑ Ⓒ Ⓓ	11.	Ⓐ Ⓑ Ⓒ Ⓓ	18.	Ⓐ Ⓑ Ⓒ Ⓓ	25.	Ⓐ Ⓑ Ⓒ Ⓓ	32.	Ⓐ Ⓑ Ⓒ Ⓓ
5.	Ⓐ Ⓑ Ⓒ Ⓓ	12.	Ⓐ Ⓑ Ⓒ Ⓓ	19.	Ⓐ Ⓑ Ⓒ Ⓓ	26.	Ⓐ Ⓑ Ⓒ Ⓓ	33.	Ⓐ Ⓑ Ⓒ Ⓓ
6.	Ⓐ Ⓑ Ⓒ Ⓓ	13.	Ⓐ Ⓑ Ⓒ Ⓓ	20.	Ⓐ Ⓑ Ⓒ Ⓓ	27.	Ⓐ Ⓑ Ⓒ Ⓓ	34.	Ⓐ Ⓑ Ⓒ Ⓓ
7.	Ⓐ Ⓑ Ⓒ Ⓓ	14.	Ⓐ Ⓑ Ⓒ Ⓓ	21.	Ⓐ Ⓑ Ⓒ Ⓓ	28.	Ⓐ Ⓑ Ⓒ Ⓓ	35.	Ⓐ Ⓑ Ⓒ Ⓓ

MODEL TEST PAPER

1. Three different positions of a triangle are given. Which of the following options describe its positions?

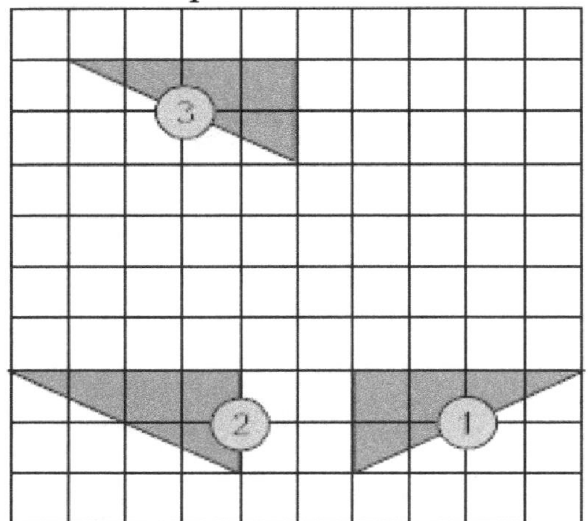

(A) Rotation, then reflection
(B) Reflection, then translation
(C) Reflection, then rotation
(D) None of these

2. In the given diagram, the girls who are athletic are indicated by which number?

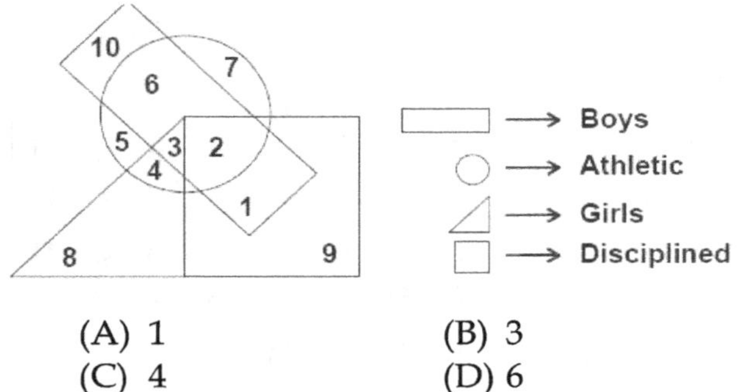

(A) 1
(C) 4
(B) 3
(D) 6

3. How many circles will be there in Pattern 20?

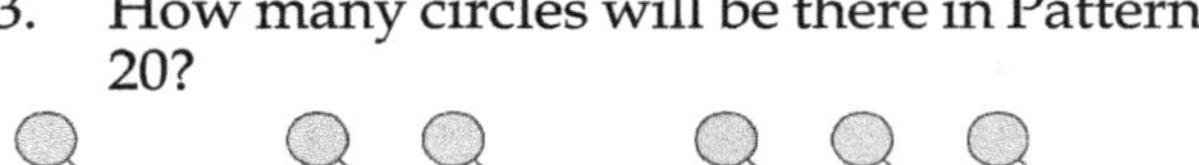

(A) 41
(B) 42
(C) 43
(D) 44

4. Raspberries cost more than Blueberries. Blueberries cost more than Strawberries. Raspberries cost more than both Strawberries and Blueberries. If the first two statements are true, the third statement is ________
(A) True
(B) False
(C) Uncertain
(D) None of these

5. Which number completes the puzzle? 25 36 49 64 81?

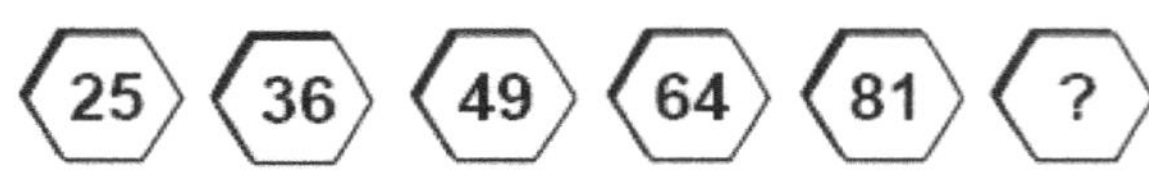

(A) 121 (B) 400
(C) 92 (D) 100

6. The water in Neha's watering bucket is boiling. What would most likely be the temperature of the water?
(A) 0°C
(B) 100°C
(C) 4°C
(D) 2°C

7. The given table shows that for science class, Mohit is ordering kits that contain bugs. Based on the data in the table, what will be the total number of bugs in 7 kits?

Bug kits

Number of kits	3	4	5	6	7
Total number of bugs	18	24	30	36	?

(A) 48   (B) 38
(C) 40   (D) 42

8. Geeta put a CD in the CD player and pressed play. When she put the CD in, it looked like the picture shown here. After the song ended, Geeta opened the CD player and the CD looked like it had rotated (turned) 90° clockwise.

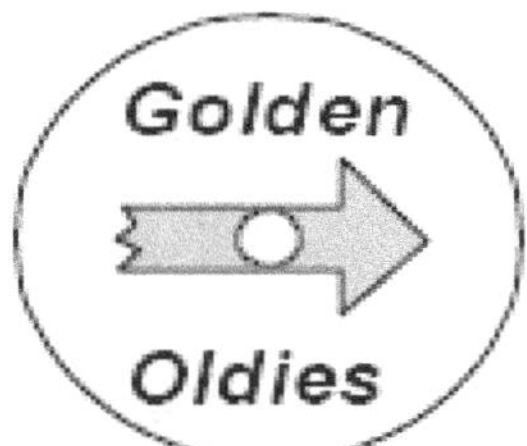

Which figure given below shows the CD after it rotated (turned) 90° clockwise?

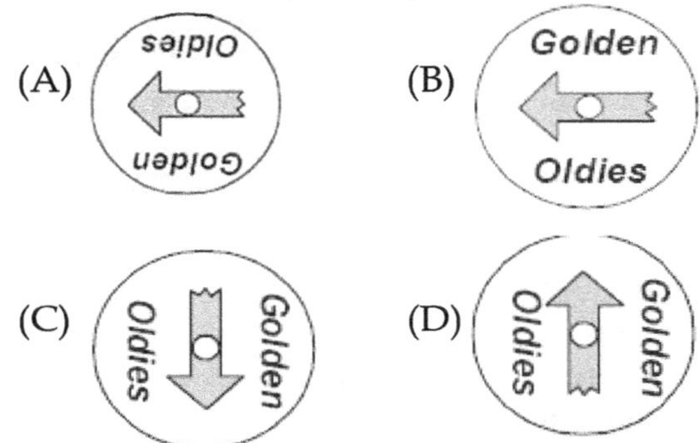

(A)   (B)   (C)   (D)

9. ? × 43 – 43 = 43 × 43 + 12 × 43

The missing number is ________?
(A) 12   (B) 54
(C) 56   (D) 98

10. Shreya has a piece of ribbon which is 2 times as long as Sasha's ribbon. If Sasha's ribbon is 8.4 m long, how much longer is Shreya's ribbon?
(A) 11.6 m   (B) 16.8 m
(C) 17.8 m   (D) 14.4 m

11. Which digit will appear on the face opposite to the face with number 1?

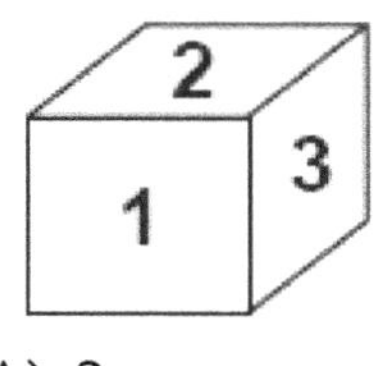

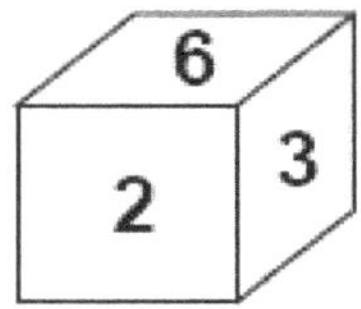

(A) 3   (B) 5
(C) 6   (D) 1

12. Which one will replace the question mark?

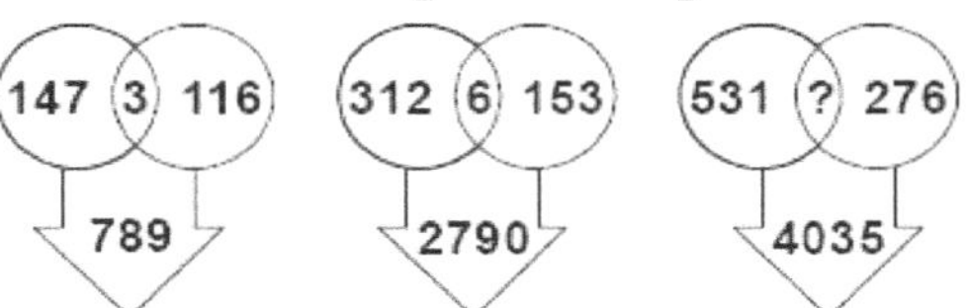

(A) 18   (B) 5
(C) 9   (D) 6

13. If "ICECREAM" is coded as "CICEERMA' then "CHOCOLATES" will be coded as
(A) OHCLOCETAS
(B) HCCOLOTASE
(C) COHOCALTES
(D) OCOHCTLASE

14. How many meaningful words can be formed using the letters A, R and T?
(A) 3   (B) 4
(C) 5   (D) 2

15. Which point is to the SouthEast of A?

(A) C   (B) B
(C) D   (D) E

16. Find the odd one out.

(A) C E D   (B) F H G
(C) I J K   (D) L N M

17. Which one of the shapes below would not look the same after half a turn?

(A)   (B)

(C)   (D)

18. Today is Wednesday. What will be the day after 94 days?

(A) Monday   (B) Tuesday
(C) Wednesday   (D) Sunday

19. John has these coins. In how many different ways can he make up a sum of 80? (You do not have to use all the coins each time)

(A) 1   (B) 3
(C) 4   (D) 6

20. What will come in the place of ? to make the number sentence true ?

24748 – ?+ 4239 × 3 = 33918

(A) 3574   (B) 3754
(C) 3457   (D) 3547

21. What should be the number in the START box?

START ⟶ ÷ 25 ⟶ – 18 = 63

(A) 2025   (B) 640
(C) 1120   (D) 207360

22. Point P is the centre of the circular target shown in the picture. Which of the following appears to be the radius of the circle?

(A) PQ
(B) SQ
(C) PR
(D) Both (A) and (C)

23. Which given figure(s) does not have a line of symmetry?

(P)   (Q)   (R)   (S)

(A) P only   (B) Q only
(C) R and S   (D) P and Q

24. The value of $15 × (17 + 19) ÷ 4 – 35 ÷ 7$ is _______

(A) 100   (B) 120
(C) 125   (D) 130

25. Peter is five times as old as his grandson, James. After six years, James will be 24 years old. How old is Peter now?

(A) 80 years   (B) 90 years
(C) 100 years   (D) 85 years

26. A watermelon is 10 times as heavy as two apples of equal mass. If the mass of each apple is 214 g, find the mass of 3 such watermelons.

(A) 12840 g   (B) 6420 g
(C) 2140 g   (D) 4280 g

27. Roman numeral for the difference of 6895 and 5287 is _______

(A) DCVIII   (B) MDCVIII
(C) MCDVIII   (D) XVICD

28. Which geometric figure has at least one triangular face?

(A) Cube   (B) Cone

(C) Cylinder   (D) Sphere

29. Tanya put one "S" on the calendar to show the date of her first basket ball game in January. Tanya's second basket ball game is exactly after 15 days. What is the date of her second basket ball game?

January

S	M	T	W	T	F	S
						1
2	3	4	5	S 6	7	8
9	10	11	12	13	14	15
16	17	18	19	20	21	22
23	24	25	26	27	28	29
30	31					

(A) 20   (B) 23

(C) 22   (D) 21

30. Akriti saw different shapes of windows on cars and trucks in a parking lot. Four of the windows she saw are drawn below.

Which window appears to have only 1 line of symmetry?

(A) Window 1   (B) Window 2

(C) Window 3   (D) Window 4

31. What is 6050.287 rounded to the nearest tenth?

(A) 6050   (B) 6100

(C) 6050.29   (D) 6050.3

32. What number am I?
- I am a two-digit even number.
- I am a common multiple of 6 and 7.
- I have a total of 8 factors.

(A) 35   (B) 42

(C) 36   (D) 84

33. When it is 10:30, what kind of angle is formed by the hands of the clock?

(A) Acute   (B) Obtuse

(C) Right   (D) Straight

34. Which point on the number line best represents 1.35?

(A) 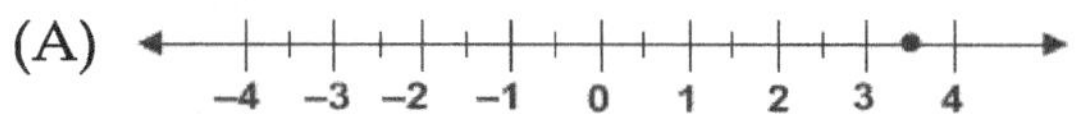

(B) 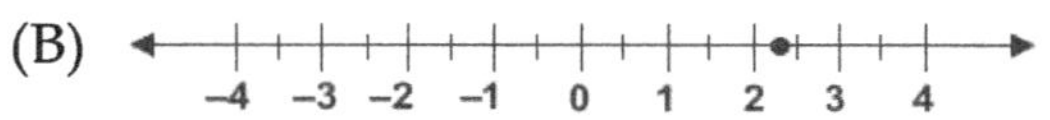

(C) 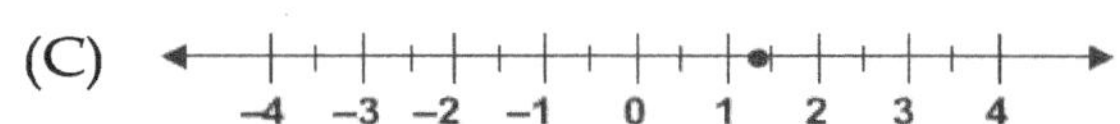

(D)

35. What is the missing value in the given pattern?

$0.25 \times 12 = 0.25 \times 3 + 0.25 \times 3 + 0.25 \times$ ____.

(A) 2   (B) 3

(C) 6   (D) 8

36. Girish is making a math puzzle. He writes that 'w' is an even number which has 12 as a factor. Which of the following could represent the variable 'w'?

(A) 2156   (B) 1728

(C) 1429   (D) 1256

37. A shopkeeper mixed 3.6 kg of hazelnuts with 0.75 kg of raisins. He packed the mixture equally into 5 boxes. What is the weight of each box?

(A) 14.25 kg   (B) 4.35 kg

(C) 0.87 kg   (D) 0.72 kg

38. Every week Suhana saves ₹ 10 on Monday and ₹ 15 on Friday. If this is her total weekly savings, how many weeks would she take to save enough to buy a ₹ 175 wireless phone?
(A) 52 weeks   (B) 46 weeks
(C) 7 weeks   (D) 14 weeks

39. There are 9 rows of seats in a theatre. Each row has the same number of seats. If there is a total of 162 seats, how many seats are in each row?
(A) 17   (B) 18
(C) 19   (D) 20

40. Arjun's snack shop sells small, medium and large sodas. Yesterday, they sold 3 large sodas and 8 more medium sodas than large sodas. Arjun's snack shop also sold 8 small sodas yesterday. Totally how many sodas did Arjun's snack shop sell yesterday?
(A) 31   (B) 13
(C) 22   (D) 33

41. Abhilasha made cake for a party. She put the cake into the oven at twenty-five past four and took it out thirty minutes later. What time was it when Abhilasha took out the cake?
(A) Five past eight   (B) Five o'clock
(C) Five to five   (D) Five past four

42. The temperature of water in a swimming pool is 51°F. Since the freezing point of water is 32°F, how many degrees would the temperature of the water have to drop to reach the freezing point?
(A) 9°F   (B) 21°F
(C) 2°F   (D) 19°F

43. There are 26 birdhouses made at a factory each hour. What is the total number of birdhouses made at the factory in 8 hours?
(A) 34   (B) 64
(C) 202   (D) 208

44. Rehana drank 5/8 glass of lemonade. Roshni drank 1/4 glass of lemonade. If the glasses held the same amount of lemonade, how much more lemonade did Rehana drink than Roshni?
(A) 3 / 8   (B) 1 /8
(C) 3 /4   (D) 1/2

45. A car can travel 315 km on 30 litres of petrol. How far can the car travel if it has 50 litres of petrol in its petrol tank?
(A) 10.5 km   (B) 189 km
(C) 525 km   (D) 840 km

———— Darken Your Choice with HB Pencil ————

1.	Ⓐ Ⓑ Ⓒ Ⓓ	10.	Ⓐ Ⓑ Ⓒ Ⓓ	19.	Ⓐ Ⓑ Ⓒ Ⓓ	28	Ⓐ Ⓑ Ⓒ Ⓓ	37. Ⓐ Ⓑ Ⓒ Ⓓ
2.	Ⓐ Ⓑ Ⓒ Ⓓ	11.	Ⓐ Ⓑ Ⓒ Ⓓ	20.	Ⓐ Ⓑ Ⓒ Ⓓ	29.	Ⓐ Ⓑ Ⓒ Ⓓ	38. Ⓐ Ⓑ Ⓒ Ⓓ
3.	Ⓐ Ⓑ Ⓒ Ⓓ	12.	Ⓐ Ⓑ Ⓒ Ⓓ	21.	Ⓐ Ⓑ Ⓒ Ⓓ	30.	Ⓐ Ⓑ Ⓒ Ⓓ	39. Ⓐ Ⓑ Ⓒ Ⓓ
4.	Ⓐ Ⓑ Ⓒ Ⓓ	13.	Ⓐ Ⓑ Ⓒ Ⓓ	22.	Ⓐ Ⓑ Ⓒ Ⓓ	31.	Ⓐ Ⓑ Ⓒ Ⓓ	40. Ⓐ Ⓑ Ⓒ Ⓓ
5.	Ⓐ Ⓑ Ⓒ Ⓓ	14.	Ⓐ Ⓑ Ⓒ Ⓓ	23.	Ⓐ Ⓑ Ⓒ Ⓓ	32.	Ⓐ Ⓑ Ⓒ Ⓓ	41. Ⓐ Ⓑ Ⓒ Ⓓ
6.	Ⓐ Ⓑ Ⓒ Ⓓ	15.	Ⓐ Ⓑ Ⓒ Ⓓ	24.	Ⓐ Ⓑ Ⓒ Ⓓ	33.	Ⓐ Ⓑ Ⓒ Ⓓ	42. Ⓐ Ⓑ Ⓒ Ⓓ
7.	Ⓐ Ⓑ Ⓒ Ⓓ	16.	Ⓐ Ⓑ Ⓒ Ⓓ	25.	Ⓐ Ⓑ Ⓒ Ⓓ	34.	Ⓐ Ⓑ Ⓒ Ⓓ	43. Ⓐ Ⓑ Ⓒ Ⓓ
8.	Ⓐ Ⓑ Ⓒ Ⓓ	17.	Ⓐ Ⓑ Ⓒ Ⓓ	26.	Ⓐ Ⓑ Ⓒ Ⓓ	35.	Ⓐ Ⓑ Ⓒ Ⓓ	44. Ⓐ Ⓑ Ⓒ Ⓓ
9.	Ⓐ Ⓑ Ⓒ Ⓓ	18.	Ⓐ Ⓑ Ⓒ Ⓓ	27.	Ⓐ Ⓑ Ⓒ Ⓓ	36.	Ⓐ Ⓑ Ⓒ Ⓓ	45. Ⓐ Ⓑ Ⓒ Ⓓ

OLYMPIAD WORKBOOK (IMO) CLASS – 5

HINTS AND SOLUTIONS

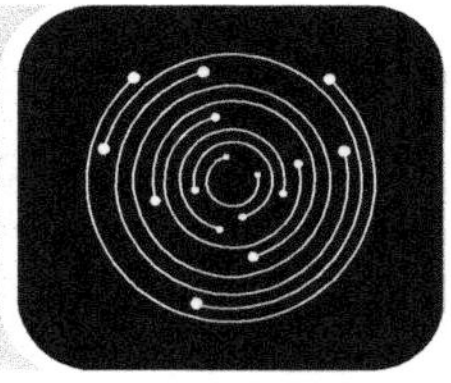

1. NUMBER SYSTEM

Answer Key

1. (C)	2. (A)	3. (A)	4. (B)	5. (C)	6. (B)	7. (B)	8. (B)	9. (B)	10. (C)
11. (B)	12. (C)	13. (B)	14. (D)	15. (B)	16. (C)	17. (D)	18. (B)	19. (B)	20. (B)

1. **(C)**

   The greatest six-digit number is 999999.

   Therefore, predecessor of the greatest six-digit number is

   999999 – 1 = 999998.

   Hence, the correct answer is (C).

2. **(A)**

   The given number is 45, 98, 351.

   $\therefore$ Place value of 5 at Lakhs place in the given number = 5 × 100000

   $\qquad\qquad = 500000$

   Place value of 5 at Tens place in the given number = 5 × 10 = 50

   $\therefore$ Difference between the place values of two 5's in the given number

   = 500000 – 50 = 499950

   Hence, the correct answer is (A).

3. **(A)**

   The given numbers are 9, 87, 61, 230 and 9, 87, 16, 230. Both these numbers have 8 digits.

   These two numbers can be written in the place value table as follows:

Crores	Ten Lakhs	Lakhs	Ten Thousands	Thousands	Hundreds	Tens	Ones
9	8	7	6	1	2	3	0
9	8	7	1	6	2	3	0

   Comparing the digits at ten thousands place, 6 > 1.

   9, 87, 61, 230 > 9, 87, 16, 230.

Therefore, the sign ">" can be placed in the box.

Hence, the correct answer is (A).

4. **(B)**

   Successor of a number is the number that comes next to the given number and it can be obtained by adding 1 to the given number.

   So, 10000001 is the successor of 10000000.

   Hence, the correct answer is (B).

5. **(C)**

   The three-digit numbers that can be formed with the digits 3, 0 and 7 are 307, 370, 703, 730.

   Thus, 4 three-digit numbers can be formed with the given digits without repetition.

   Hence, the correct answer is (C).

6. **(B)**

   The given numbers can be placed in the place value table as follows:

Lakhs	Ten thousands	Thousands	Hundreds	Tens	Ones
3	2	1	9	8	7
3	1	9	2	4	0
3	2	1	9	7	8
3	2	1	9	7	0

   It can be observed that the digits at lakhs place are the same.

   On comparing the digits at ten thousands place, we get 2 > 1.

   $\therefore$ 319240 is smallest amongst the given numbers.

Consider the numbers 321987, 321978 and 321970.

Here, the digits at thousands place are the same.

Also, the digits at hundreds place are the same.

On comparing the digits at tens place, we get 8 > 7.

∴ 321987 > (321978, 321970)

Therefore, among the given numbers, 321987 and 319240 are the greatest and smallest numbers respectively

Hence, the correct answer is (B).

7. (B)

The given digits are 3, 0, 9, 1 and 5.

The greatest 5-digit number formed by using all the given digits is 95310.

The smallest 5-digit number formed by using all the given digits is 10359.

∴ Required difference
= 95310 – 10359 = 84951

Hence, the correct answer is (B).

8. (B)

It is known that 1 million = 10 lakh and 1 crore = 100 lakh

∴ 1 crore = 10 × 10 lakh = 10 million

So, 3 crore = 3 × 10 million
            = 30 million

Therefore, 30 millions is equal to 3 crore.

Hence, the correct answer is (B).

9. (B)

Fifty million twenty-one thousand two hundred and thirty-six can be written in International system of numeration as 50,021,236.

This number can be rewritten in Indian system of numeration as 5,00,21,236.

Hence, the correct answer is (B).

10. (C)

1 billion = 1000 million
and 1 million = 1000 thousands

It is known that

1000 > 10, 10000 > 216

∴ 1000 million > 10 million, 10000 million > 216 million

So, 1 billion > 10 million, 10 million > 216 thousand

∴ 1 billion > 10 million > 216 thousand

Thus, the given numbers can be arranged in descending order as

1 billion, 10 million, 216 thousands

Hence, the correct answer is (C).

11. (B)

The numbers 2,357,822 and 2,357,799 can be placed in place value table as

Million	Hundred thousands	Ten thousands	Thousands	Hundreds	Tens	Ones
2	3	5	7	8	2	2
2	3	5	7	7	9	9

It is seen that the digits at million, hundred thousands, ten thousands and thousands place are the same.

Comparing the digits at hundreds place, 8 > 7.

Thus, 2,357,822 > 2,357,799

Hence, the correct answer is B.

12. (B)

It is known that 1 million = 1,000,000

35 million = 35,000,000

Therefore, there are six zeroes in 35 million.

Hence, the correct answer is (C).

13. (B)

18 is composite because 18 can be written as a product of factors, other than 1 and 18 :

18 = 2 × 9 or 18 = 3 × 6.

19 is prime because 19 doesn't have any factors except 1 and 19.

20 is composite because 20 can be written as a product of factors, other than 1 and 20 :

20 = 2 × 10 or 20 = 4 × 5

21 is composite because 21 can be written as a product of factors, other than 1 and 21 : 21 = 3 × 7

14. (D)

26 is composite because 26 can be written as a product of factors, other than 1 and 26 :

26 = 2 × 13.

27 is composite because 27 can be written as a product of factors, other than 1 and 27:

27 = 3 × 3 × 3 or 3^3

28 is composite because 28 can be written as a product of factors, other than 1 and 28:

28 = 4 × 7 or 2^2 × 7.

29 is prime because 29 doesn't have any factors except 1 and 29.

15. **(B)**

69 is composite number. 67, 71 and 73 are all prime numbers.

16. **(C)**

105 = 3 × 35 or 3 × 5 × 7, and so is composite.

101, 103 and 107 are all prime numbers.

17. **(D)**

2 and 3 are prime numbers; 4, 6 and 8 are composite numbers.

All the products are correct, but only answer (D) is a product of prime factors.

18. **(B)**

2, 3 and 5 are prime numbers; 6, 9 and 15 are composite numbers.

All the products are correct, but only answer (B) has a product of prime factors.

19. **(B)**

Place value of 5 is 5 × 10 = 50. So, answer is (B).

20. **(B)**

Place value of 5 in

750 = 5 × 10 = 50
17510 = 5 × 100 = 500
124605 = 5 × 1 = 5
50630 = 5 × 10000 = 50000

So, answer is (B).

HOTS (ACHIEVERS SECTION)

21. (B)	22. (B)	23. (C)	24. (C)	25. (D)

2. COMPUTATION OPERATIONS

Answer Key

1. (C)	2. (A)	3. (D)	4. (C)	5. (C)	6. (D)	7. (C)	8. (B)	9. (C)	10. (C)
11. (B)	12. (B)	13. (A)	14. (A)	15. (A)	16. (B)	17. (C)	18. (B)	19. (A)	20. (A)
21. (A)	22. (A)	23. (C)	24. (C)	25. (B)	26. (C)	27. (A)	28. (B)	29. (C)	30. (C)

3. **(D)**

3396 = 3000 + 300 + 90 + 6
= MMMCCCXCVI

5. **(C)**

2,011 = 2,000 + 10 + 1
2,000 = MM, 10 = X and 1 = I
So 2,011 = MMXI

6. **(D)**

7,192 = 7,000 + 100 + 90 + 2

7,000 = MMMMMMM, 100 = C, 90 = XC and 2 = II

So 7,192 = MMMMMMMCXCII

12. **(B)**

We have,

$$\begin{array}{r} 4132 \\ \times\ 27 \\ \hline 28924 \\ 8264\times \\ \hline 111564 \end{array}$$

13. (A)
728189.901

16. (B)
Here, $(15 \times 3) \div 5 \times 8 - 2 + 6 \, (8 - 2)$
$= 45 \div 5 \times 8 - 2 + 6 \times 6$
$= 72 - 2 + 36 = 106$

17. (C)
Both are equal. Hence $i = ii$

19. (A)
Required No. of bulbs = 13780 × 278
$= 3830840$

20. (A)
Other number $= 882\overline{)127008}(144$

21. (A)
Required number = H.C.F. of (91 – 43), (183 – 91) and (183 – 43) = H.C.F. of 48, 92 and 140 = 4.

22. (A)
Factors are numbers that can be divided exactly into another number.

23. (C)
Clearly, the numbers are (23 × 13) and (23 × 14). Larger number = (23 × 14) = 322.

24. (C)
All of the numbers (2, 5, 10) in this set divide 10 exactly.

25. (B)
All of the numbers (2, 8, 4) in this set divide 16 exactly.

26. (C)
5620 as this number is a multiple of 2.

27. (A)
N = H.C.F. of (4665 – 1305), (6905 – 4665) and (6905 - 1305) = H.C.F. of 3360, 2240 and 5600 = 1120.
Sum of digits in N = (1 + 1 + 2 + 0) = 4

28. (B)
1985 as this is a multiple of 5 because it ends in a 5.

29. (C)
$4 \times 5 = 20$.

30. (C)
The multiples of 6 are: 6, 12, 18, 24, 30, ...
The multiples of 8 are: 8, 16, 24, 32, ...
The least common multiple of 6 and 8 is 24.

HOTS (ACHIEVERS SECTION)

31. (D)	32. (B)	33. (B)	34. (B)	35. (C)

3. DECIMALS AND FRACTIONS

Answer Key

1. (D)	2. (B)	3. (C)	4. (B)	5. (D)	6. (C)	7. (A)	8. (A)	9. (C)	10. (A)
11. (D)	12. (C)	13. (B)	14. (B)	15. (C)	16. (A)	17. (A)	18. (B)	19. (C)	20. (C)
21. (D)	22. (C)	23. (A)	24. (C)	25. (B)					

7. (A)
The hundredths digit is the second digit to the right of the decimal point, which is 1

8. (A)
The tenths place comes immediately after the decimal point and the hundredths place comes after that. In this case the digit in the tenths place is 7 and the digit in the hundredths place is 2

12. (C)
The lowest place value in the number is the ten-thousandths, but that's not

what the question is asking. The smallest digit in the number is 2, which is in the thousandths place: 489.6327

15. (C)

9 is the third digit to the right of the decimal point, so it is 9 thousandths.(2 is in the tenths place, 4 is in the hundredths place, 9 is in the thousandths place and 5 is in the ten-thousandths place)

16. (A)

The tenths digit is the first digit to the right of the decimal point, which is the 7.

19. (C)

6 is the first digit to the right of the decimal point, so it is 6 tenths.

20. (C)

The highest place value in the number is the thousands, but that's not what the question is asking. The largest digit in the number is 9, which is in the tenths place.

21. (D)

There are 7 slices of pizza left on the plate out of eight pieces altogether. Therefore, the fraction of pizza shown is 7/8.

22. (C)

The diagram shows 5 slices of pizza left on the plate out of eight slices altogether. So the fraction is 5/8. The numerator is the top number, which is 5.

23. (A)

The denominator is the number on the bottom of the fraction. To get an equivalent fraction with denominator 12, we have to multiply the denominator (3) by 4. Therefore, we also have to multiply the numerator (2) by 4 and we get 8/12.

24. (C)

The fractions are all equivalent to 2/5 except the odd one out, which is 9/20, because when you multiply denominator and numerator by 4 you get 8/20.

HOTS (ACHIEVERS SECTION)				
26. (B)	27. (D)	28. (B)	29. (B)	30. (B)

4. MEASUREMENT

Answer Key

1. (B)	2. (B)	3. (C)	4. (A)	5. (D)	6. (C)	7. (A)	8. (C)	9. (B)	10. (A)
11. (D)	12. (B)	13. (B)	14. (C)	15. (A)	16. (D)	17. (B)	18. (C)	19. (A)	20. (A)
21. (A)	22. (B)	23. (B)	24. (C)	25. (B)	26. (C)	27. (C)	28. (B)	29. (A)	30. (D)

11. (D)

Correct answer is (D)

12. (B)

First $32° \times \dfrac{9}{5} = \dfrac{288°}{5} = 57.6°$

Then: $57.6° + 32° = 89.6°F$

13. (B)

Correct answer is (B)

14. (C)

Correct answer is (C)

15. (A)

First: $11° \times \dfrac{9}{5} = \dfrac{99°}{5} = 19.8°$

Then: $19.8° + 32° = 51.8°F$

16. (D)

First: 68° – 32° = 36°

Then: $36 \times \dfrac{5}{9} = \dfrac{180°}{9} = 20°C$

17. (B)

First: 18° – 32° = –14°

Then $-14° \times \dfrac{5}{9} = \dfrac{-70°}{9} = -7.8°$

(to 1 dec place)

18. (C)

First: $57.8° \times \dfrac{9}{5} = \dfrac{520.2°}{5} = 104.04°$

Then: 104.04° + 32° = 136.04°F. This is 136°F to the nearest degree

19. (A)

First: 101.3° – 32° = 69.3°

Then: $69.3° \times \dfrac{5}{9} = \dfrac{346.5°}{9} = 38.5°$

20. (A)

(41 °F – 32) × (5/9)
$= 9 \times (5/9) = 5 ° C$

21. (A)

Required amount

= [2 × 5 + 4 × 10 + 3 × 50 + 2 × 500] – 1162
= [10 + 40 + 150 + 1000] – 1162
= 1200 – 1162
= ₹ 38

22. (B)

Price of one cookie = 6.6
= ₹ 6.60

23. (B)

Total amount Ankit needs to pay

$= \dfrac{180}{2} + \dfrac{15}{3} = 90 + 5 = 95$

25. (B)

Price of two chocolates $= \dfrac{15}{3} \times 2$

= 10

Hence given statement is not correct.

26. (C)

Price of one chocolate $= \dfrac{15}{3} = 5$

∴ Manpreet can buy

$= \dfrac{122}{5} = 24.4$

= 24 chocolates

29. (A)

Total amount spent by Shraddha and Shubhra together in shopping
= (550 + 275 + 50) + (250 + 480 + 115 + 500)
= 875 + 1345 = ₹ 2220

30. (D)

Amount left with Shubhra after shopping
= 2000 – 1345 = 655

HOTS (ACHIEVERS SECTION)

31. (D)	32. (D)	33. (A)	34. (D)	35. (B)

5. ALGEBRA

Answer Key

1. (A)	2. (B)	3. (A)	4. (D)	5. (C)	6. (B)	7. (D)	8. (A)	9. (C)	10. (C)
11. (D)	12. (B)	13. (B)	14. (A)	15. (A)					

| 16. (C) | 17. (A) | 18. (B) | 19. (C) | 20. (B) |

6. GEOMETRICAL SHAPES AND ANGLES

Answer Key

1. (B)	2. (A)	3. (D)	4. (A)	5. (B)	6. (C)	7. (D)	8. (B)	9. (D)	10. (C)
11. (B)	12. (C)	13. (C)	14. (A)	15. (C)	16. (C)	17. (C)	18. (A)	19. (D)	20. (A)
21. (B)	22. (D)	23. (B)	24. (C)	25. (B)					

1. **(B)**
   The middle letter is where the angle actually is (its vertex), which is D. Therefore we could write the angle as ∠BDA or ∠ADB.

2. **(A)**
   The middle letter is where the angle actually is (its vertex), which is C. Therefore we could write the angle as ∠BCD or ∠DCB.

3. **(D)**
   An acute angle is less than 90°.
   If you add two acute angles then
   (*i*) the sum could be acute, example:
      10° + 20° = 30° (an acute angle).
   (*ii*) the sum could be right, example:
      40° + 50° = 90° (a right angle).
   (*iii*) the sum could be obtuse, example:
      30° + 80° = 110° (an obtuse angle).
   (*iv*) the sum could NOT be straight because each acute angle is less than 90° and a straight angle is 180°, example:
      89° + 89° = 178° which is less than a straight angle.

4. **(A)**
   An acute angle is less than 90° i.e. it is less than a right angle. Half a right angle (45°) is less than a right angle, so it is acute.

5. **(B)**
   The following angles are all less than 90°, so are acute:
   ∠AOB, ∠BOC, ∠COD, ∠DOE, ∠AOC, ∠AOD, ∠BOD, ∠BOE and ∠COE
   Therefore there are 9 acute angles altogether. Note that ∠AOE is obtuse.

6. **(C)**
   Each of the five triangles at the points of the pentagram has three acute angles. So there are 5 × 3 = 15 acute angles altogether in the pentagram. (All other angles are not acute)

7. **(D)**
   The marked angles are all less than 90°, so are acute :

   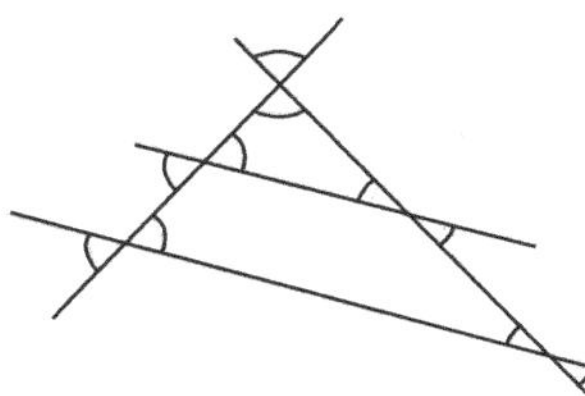

   Therefore there are 10 acute angles altogether.

8. **(B)**
   The angles marked with arcs are all less than 90°, so are acute. The four angles around the top point are all right angles. So there are 10 acute angles altogether.

   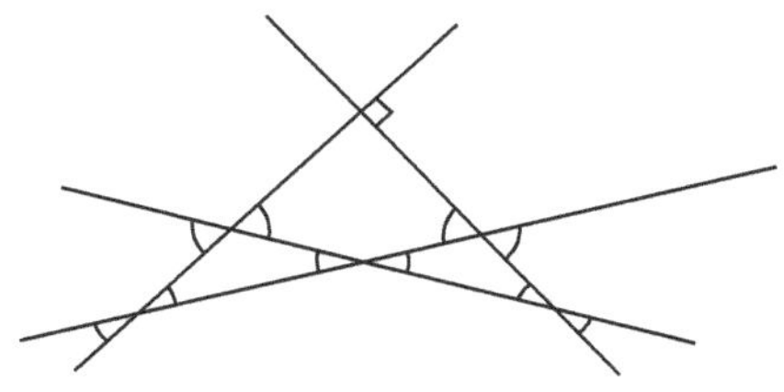

9. **(D)**

Because one pair of lines is parallel (that is what the two arrows mean) and the other two lines are perpendicular to them (the little boxes mean right angles), the shape inside the four lines must be a rectangle. And there are 4 right angles at each of the four points where lines intersect. So there are 4 × 4 = 16 right angles altogether.

10. **(C)**

A full rotation consists of four right angles. So two full rotations consist of eight right angles.

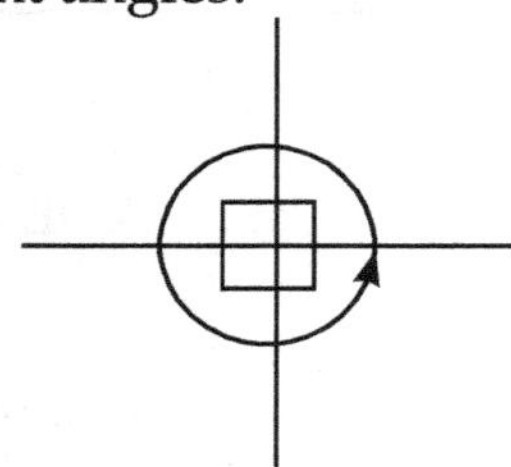

11. **(B)**

The following angles are obtuse :
∠AOD, ∠AOE, ∠AOF, ∠BOD, ∠BOE, ∠BOF, ∠COE and ∠COF. Therefore, there are 8 obtuse angles altogether.

12. **(C)**

Half a right angle = 45°
One right angle = 90°
One and a half right angles
= 1½ × 90° = 135°
Two right angles = 180°
Only 135° is greater than 90° but less than 180°, so it is the only obtuse angle.

13. **(C)**

A full rotation consists of two straight (180°) angles. So three full rotations consist of six straight angles.

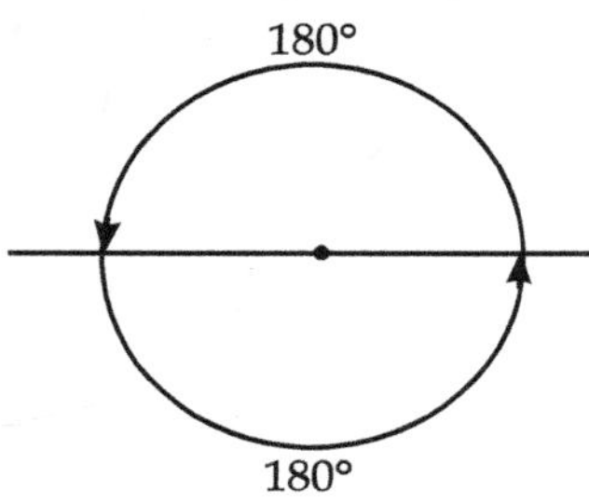

14. **(A)**

A reflex angle is more than 180° but less than 360°. 178° is less than 180°, so it is not reflex. (All the rest are reflex angles.)

15. **(C)**

A Reflex Angle is greater than 180° but less than 360°. A, B and D are all less than 180°. Only C is greater than 180° but less than 360°.

16. **(C)**

If you add the smaller angle (acute or obtuse) and the reflex angle for the same shape you will always come to 360°. Therefore, reflex angle AOB
= 360° − 67° = 293°

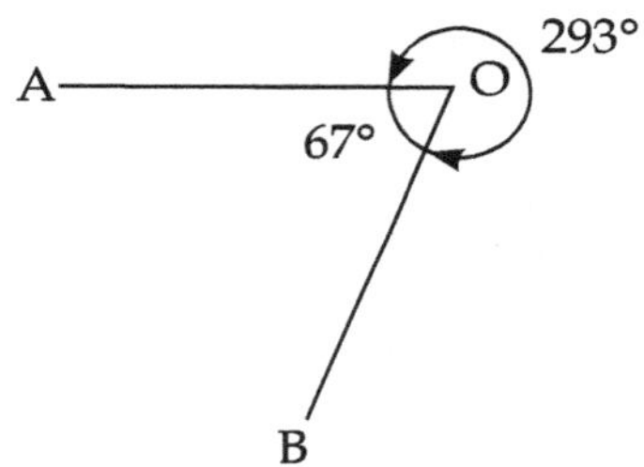

17. **(C)**

$2 × 33° = 66°$, which is between 0° and 90°, so acute.

$5 × 33° = 165°$, which is between 90° and 180°, so obtuse.

$6 × 33° = 198°$, which is between 180° and 360°, so reflex.

$7 × 33° = 231°$, which is also reflex, but we have already found the least amount which is 6.

18. **(A)**

The triangle has three different lengths of side, so is scalene. The triangle has lengths 3, 4 and 5 and $5^2 = 3^2 + 4^2$, so is right angled. Therefore, it is a scalene right angled triangle.

19. **(D)**

Since the triangle is isosceles, it must have two equal angles. Since it is also right angled, the other two angles must both be 45° (45° + 45° +90° = 180°)

So (A) is true.

Since the triangle is isosceles, it must have two of its sides equal.

So (B) is true.

An isosceles triangle has one line of symmetry.

So (C) is also true.

A triangle that satisfies A, B and C is shown in the following diagram:

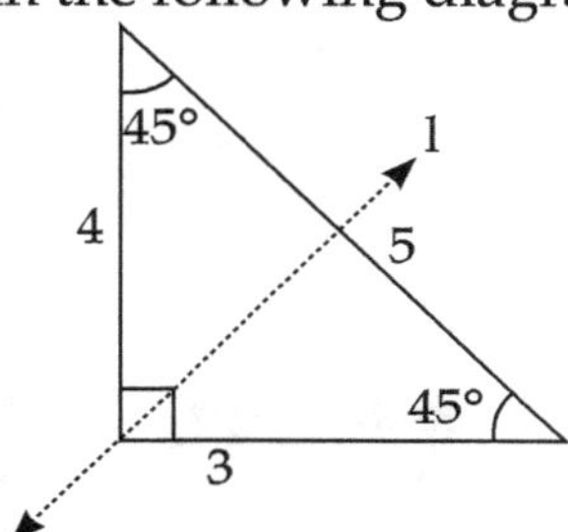

Line l is the axis of symmetry

Statement (D) must be false since a triangle with three different sides cannot be isosceles.

20. (A)

Shraddha could make an isosceles triangle, a parallelogram, a rectangle or a kite :

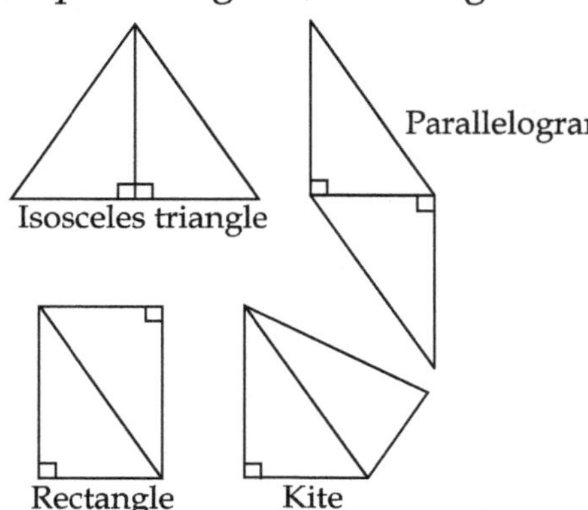

But the rectangle is not a square because the sides have different lengths.

21. (B)

Shraddha could make a square, an isosceles triangle (one with 2 equal sides, 2 equal angles), and a parallelogram:

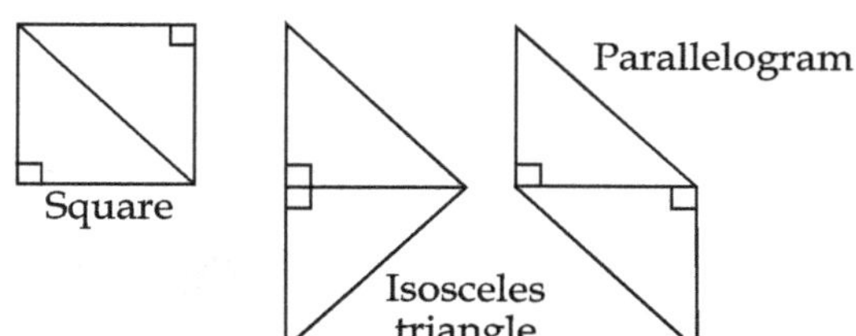

But she could not make an equilateral triangle (one with all equal sides, all equal angles).

22. (D)

If it's a complete turn, then the square will finish in the same position that it started, so the answer is (D).

23. (B)

It has 4 lines of symmetry

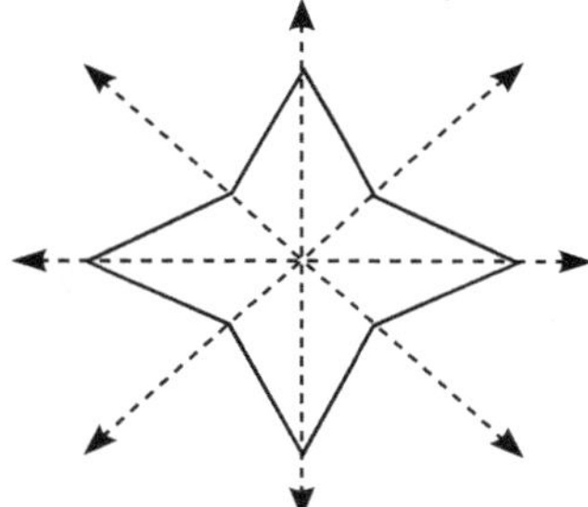

24. (C)

The star has seven points and is symmetrical. Therefore its order of rotational symmetry is 7.

25. (B)

It does not look the same after a rotation of 45° :

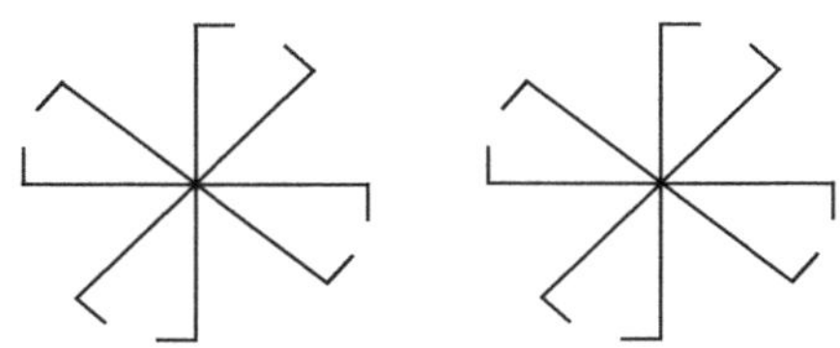

after a 45° rotation

It requires a rotation of 90° before it looks the same. So it looks the same after rotations of 90°, 180°, 270° and 360° takes it back to its original position. So the order of rotational symmetry is 4

26. (C)	27. (B)	28. (C)	29. (C)	30. (C)

7. AREA, PERIMETER AND VOLUME

Answer Key

1. (B)	2. (C)	3. (B)	4. (D)	5. (A)	6. (D)	7. (C)	8. (B)	9. (C)	10. (A)
11. (A)	12. (C)	13. (A)	14. (B)	15. (C)	16. (D)	17. (D)	18. (A)	19. (C)	20. (A)

HOTS [ACHIEVERS SECTION

21. (C)	22. (A)	23. (D)	24. (C)	25. (C)

8. SYMMETRY

Answer Key

1. (A)	2. (B)	3. (A)	4. (B)	5. (A)	6. (A)	7. (B)	8. (A)	9. (B)	10. (A)
11. (C)	12. (D)	13. (C)	14. (A)	15. (B)	16. (D)	17. (B)	18. (D)	19. (B)	20. (B)

13. (C)

C is the line of symmetry that divides into two perfectly identical halves.

14. (A)

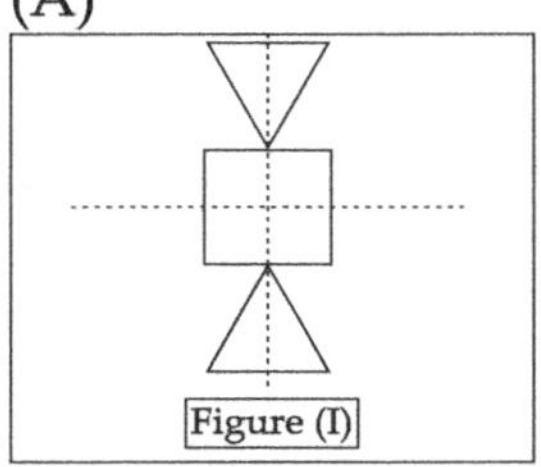

Figure (I)

A and B are the lines of symmetry. There are two lines of symmetry in Figure (I).

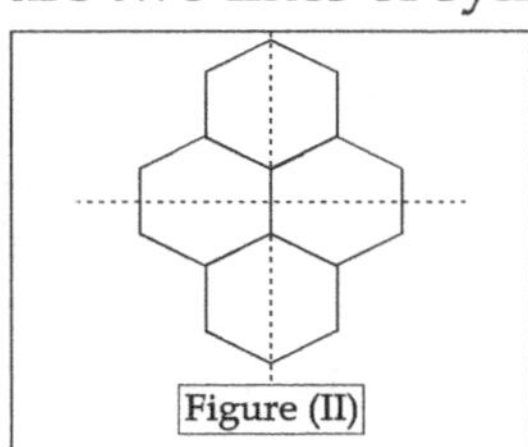

Figure (II)

P and Q are the lines of symmetry. There are two lines of symmetry in Figure (II).

They have an equal number of lines of symmetry. Hence, their difference is zero.

15. (B)

Number of squares that must be added so that the line PQ becomes a line of symmetry is shown as.

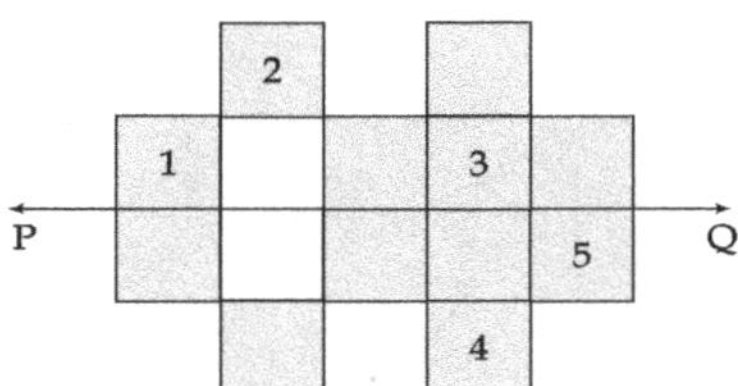

The least number of squares that must be added so that the line PQ becomes a line of symmetry is 5.

16. (D)

The order of rotational symmetry of an equilateral triangle is 3 and its angle of rotation is 120° which is shown as:

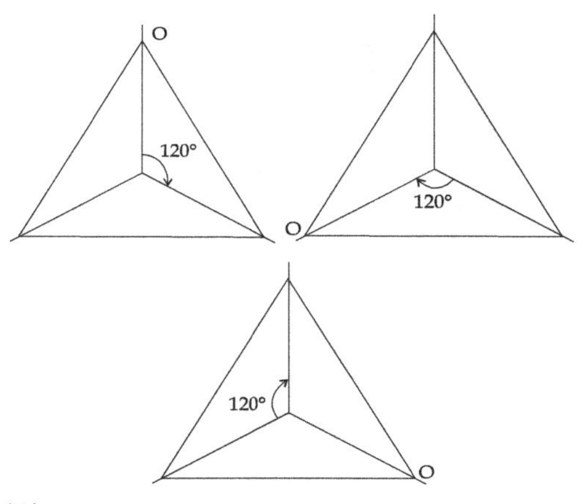

17. (B)

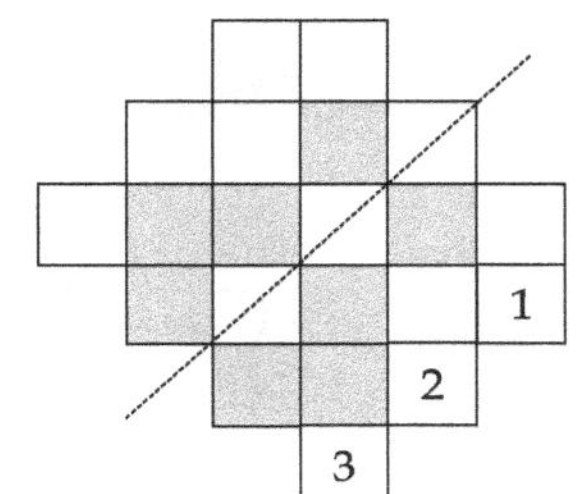

20. (B)

<table>
<tr><th colspan="5">HOTS (ACHIEVERS SECTION)</th></tr>
<tr><td>21. (B)</td><td>22. (B)</td><td>23. (C)</td><td>24. (A)</td><td>25. (A)</td></tr>
</table>

21. (B)

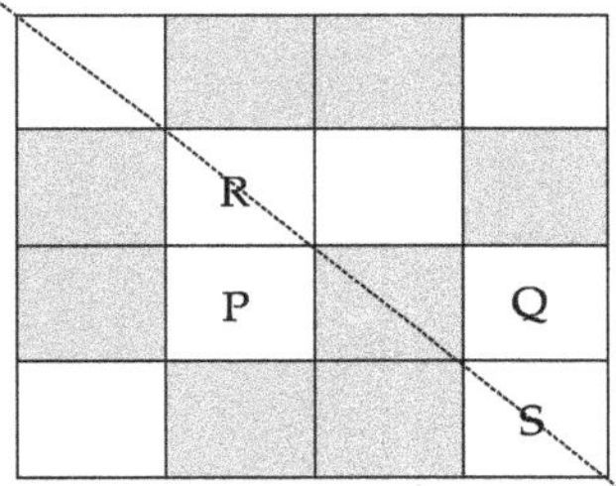

22. (B)

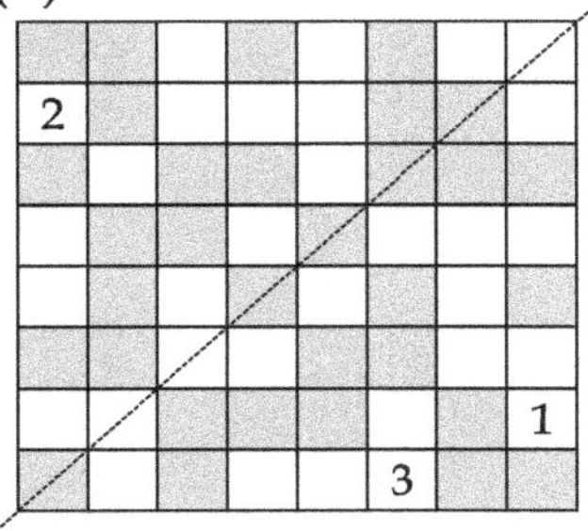

23. (C)

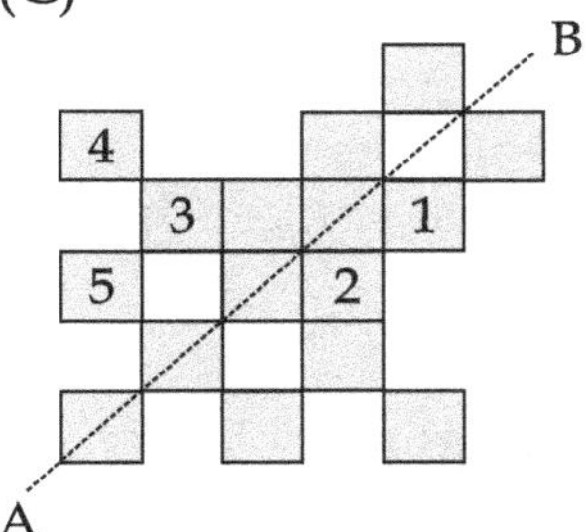

Answer Key

1. (B)	2. (C)	3. (B)	4. (D)	5. (C)	6. (A)	7. (B)	8. (C)	9. (C)	10. (A)
11. (D)	12. (B)	13. (B)	14. (B)	15. (C)	16. (D)	17. (C)	18. (C)	19. (B)	20. (B)

1. (B)

The number of sixes is given by its frequency, or how high the bar is for the score 6. So, look for 6 across the horizontal axis and then read off its frequency on the vertical axis. There were 3 sixes.

2. (C)

5 of them favored orange and only 1 favored green. $5 - 1 = 4$ Therefore 4 more favored orange than those who favored green.

3. (B)

Shraddha's best subject was English, where she scored 60. Shraddha's worst subject was Geography, where she scored 25. Therefore she scored $(60 - 25) = 35$ more in her best subject than in her worst subject.

4. (D)

The top of the English column on the graph is mapped to the point 60 on the vertical axis. So, Shraddha's score for English was 60. Then, we must add 15% of 60 to 60 to get Shubhra's score for English. $60 + (15\%)(60)$

$= 60 + 9 = 69$.

5. (C)

Sleep represents 25% of Shraddha's day. 25% of 24 hours

$$= \tfrac{1}{4} \times 24 \text{ hours}$$

$$= 6 \text{ hours.}$$

So the height of the bar for sleep would be 6 hours.

6. (A)

She spent about 8.5 hours sleeping and about 4.9 hours watching TV.

$$8.5 - 4.9 = 3.6$$

That's about 3½ hours longer.

8. (C)

From the information shown in the graph, the record remained unchanged from 1968 to 1980 - a 12 year period. (In fact it remained unchanged for nearly 15 years from October 1968 to July 1983)

10. (a)

The number of students that were greater than or equal to 55 inches tall but less than 70 inches tall are shown in the bars representing the groups 55 - 60, 60 - 65 and 65 - 70

$= 6 + 5 + 2$

$= 13$

12. (B)

2 babies or 2% had a low birth weight. 7 babies or 7% had a high birth weight.

Therefore $100\% - (2\% + 7\%) = 91\%$ of the babies had neither a low nor a high birth weight.

13. (B)

The correct answer is (B). Construct a Frequency Distribution table as follow:

Letter	Tally	Frequency
A	| |	2
E	| | |	4
H	| |	2

I			1
L			1
N	||	2
S	|||||	5
T	||||	4
U			1
W	||	2
Y			1

The letter that occurs the most frequently is S.

14. (B)

The correct answer is (B). Scores less than 3 means 1 or 2, and does not include 3 itself. There were 16 1's and 18 2's, so 34 altogether less than 3.

15. (C)

The correct answer is (C). 5 or more includes 5, 6, 7, 8, 9 and 10. The sum of the frequencies for these scores

= 11 + 8 + 7 + 4 + 1 + 2 = 33

16. (D)

The right answer is (D). Greater than or equal to 4, but less than or equal to 7 includes 4, 5, 6 and 7.

    8 students scored 4

    11 students scored 5

    8 students scored 6

    7 students scored 7

So 8 + 11 + 8 + 7 = 34 scored greater than or equal to 4, but less than or equal to 7.

17. (C)

The right answer is (C). Less than 3 includes 0, 1 and 2, but does not include 3.

    4 classmates had 0 pets

    12 classmates had 1 pet

    8 classmates had 2 pets

So, 4 + 12 + 8 = 24 had less than 3 pets.

18. (C)

The correct answer is (C). There is a trick to this question. The table shows the number of siblings (brother and sister) each child has. The question asks how many children in the family ... which also includes the child being surveyed. So if a child has 3 siblings, then the family has 4 children!

So to find How many families had more than 4 children, we must include those children with 4, 5, 6, 7, 8 and 9 siblings:

4 of them had 4 siblings

2 of them had 5 siblings

1 of them had 6 siblings

0 of them had 7 siblings

0 of them had 8 siblings

1 of them had 9 siblings

So 4 + 2 + 1 + 0 + 0 + 1 = 8 of them came from families with more than 4 children.

19. (B)

is discrete because the numbers of brothers and sisters can only be values like 0, 1, 2 etc. The other three are all continuous because they can take any value within a range, such as 160.3 cm or 75.35 kg.

20. (B)

Total cars 2 + 4 + 6 + 5 + 2 = 19

HOTS (ACHIEVERS SECTION)

| 21. (B) | 22. (D) | 23. (C) | 24. (B) | 25. (C) |

Answer Key

1. (B)	2. (C)	3. (C)	4. (C)	5. (C)	6. (D)	7. (C)	8. (B)	9. (D)	10. (A)
11. (B)	12. (D)	13. (B)	14. (D)	15. (C)	16. (C)	17. (A)	18. (C)	19. (B)	20. (B)
21. (C)	22. (E)	23. (B)	24. (C)	25. (C)	26. (A)	27. (C)	28. (B)	29. (D)	30. (B)
31. (D)	32. (B)	33. (D)	34. (C)	35. (D)					

1. (B)
    The first numbers increase by 5, 7, 9, 11.... The letters move one step backward. The last numbers are consecutive odd numbers.

2. (C)
    The first letter of the terms are alternate. The sequence followed by the numbers is +2, +3, +4,.... The last letter is three steps ahead of the last letter of the preceding term.

3. (C)
    The first letters in odd numbered terms from series J, I, H and in even numbered terms from the series K, L, M. The sequence followed by the numbers is + 2, + 3, + 4, + 5, + 6. The third letter moves two steps backward.

4. (C)
    The letters move 1, 2, 3, ... steps forward. The numbers increase by + 3, + 5, + 7, + 9....

5. (C)
    The letters are alternate and the numbers indicate their position in the alphabet from the beginning.

6. (D)
    Anthropology deals with the study of man. Similarly, anthology deals with collection of poems

7. (C)
    First is the noise produced by the second.

8. (B)
    Second is the manner of walking of the first.

9. (D) Light rays falling on a mirror undergoes reflection and those falling on water undergoes refraction.

10. (A)
    The words in each pair are antonyms of each other.

11. (B)
    Only rubber is a tree product.

13. (B)
    All others are sounds made by animals or birds.

14. (D)
    All other items are metals.

15. (C)
    Except 'Litre' all others represent the unit to measure length.

16. (C)

Here	G	I	V	E
	↓	↓	↓	↓
	5	1	3	7
and	B	A	T	
	↓	↓	↓	
	9	2	4	
then	G	A	T	E
	↓	↓	↓	↓
	5	2	4	7

17. (A)

The first letter of the word (LUTE) is moved one step forward to obtain the first letter of the code, while the other letters remain unaltered.

18. (C)

Letters of the word INSTITUTION have been just reversed in the coded word. Hence PERFECTION will be coded as NOITCEFREP

19. (B)

First three letters of the word are kept as it is, sixth letter comes at fourth place shifting fourth and fifth letters to fifth and sixth placed respectively, and last two letters are exchanged.

20. (B)

Letters at odd place in the coded word are one letter ahead of the letters in the basic word and letters at even places are one letter behind the letters in the basic word as their positions in the alphabet.

21. (C)

Letters in the given word	Letters in the alphabetical order
S T	S T
R O P	R Q P
O P	O P

22. (E)

Letters in the given word	Letters in the alphabetical order
S E Q	S R Q
Q U E N	Q P O N
S E Q U E N	S R Q P O N
E N T I A	E D C B A

23. (B)

Letters in the given word	Letters in the alphabetical order
P U R	P Q R

24. (C)

Letters in the given word	Letters in the alphabetical order
P R E S	P Q R S
R E S E N	R Q P O N

25. (C)

Letters in the given word	Letters in the alphabetical order
D E	D E
Q U A T	Q R S T
Q U A T E L	Q P O N M L

MODEL TEST PAPER

Answer Key

1. (B)	2. (C)	3. (A)	4. (A)	5. (D)	6. (B)	7. (D)	8. (C)	9. (C)	10. (B)
11. (C)	12. (B)	13. (B)	14. (A)	15. (A)	16. (C)	17. (D)	18. (D)	19. (C)	20. (D)
21. (A)	22. (D)	23. (D)	24. (D)	25. (B)	26. (A)	27. (B)	28. (B)	29. (C)	30. (D)
31. (D)	32. (B)	33. (B)	34. (C)	35. (C)	36. (B)	37. (C)	38. (C)	39. (B)	40. (C)
41. (C)	42. (D)	43. (D)	44. (A)	45. (C)					

SAMPLE OMR ANSWER SHEET

1. STUDENT NAME (IN ENGLISH CAPITAL LETTERS ONLY)

Students must write and darken the respective circles completely using HB Pencil only. Othewise their Answer Sheets will not be evaluated.

PERSONAL DETAILS

2. SCHOOL CODE

3. CLASS

4. SECTION

5. ROLL NO.

6. QUESTION PAPER SET

A ○
B ○
C ○
D ○

7. MOBILE NUMBER

8. GENDER

MALE ○
FEMALE ○

9. STREAM
(Only for Class XI and XII Students)

MATHEMATICS ○
BIOLOGY ○
OTHERS ○

MARK YOUR ANSWERS

No.	A	B	C	D	No.	A	B	C	D
1.	A	B	C	D	26.	A	B	C	D
2.	A	B	C	D	27.	A	B	C	D
3.	A	B	C	D	28.	A	B	C	D
4.	A	B	C	D	29.	A	B	C	D
5.	A	B	C	D	30.	A	B	C	D
6.	A	B	C	D	31.	A	B	C	D
7.	A	B	C	D	32.	A	B	C	D
8.	A	B	C	D	33.	A	B	C	D
9.	A	B	C	D	34.	A	B	C	D
10.	A	B	C	D	35.	A	B	C	D
11.	A	B	C	D	36.	A	B	C	D
12.	A	B	C	D	37.	A	B	C	D
13.	A	B	C	D	38.	A	B	C	D
14.	A	B	C	D	39.	A	B	C	D
15.	A	B	C	D	40.	A	B	C	D
16.	A	B	C	D	41.	A	B	C	D
17.	A	B	C	D	42.	A	B	C	D
18.	A	B	C	D	43.	A	B	C	D
19.	A	B	C	D	44.	A	B	C	D
20.	A	B	C	D	45.	A	B	C	D
21.	A	B	C	D	46.	A	B	C	D
22.	A	B	C	D	47.	A	B	C	D
23.	A	B	C	D	48.	A	B	C	D
24.	A	B	C	D	49.	A	B	C	D
25.	A	B	C	D	50.	A	B	C	D

Signature of the Student & Date of Examination

Signature of the Invigilator & Date of Examination

V&S Publishers, F-2/16 Ansari Road, Daryaganj, New Delhi-110002, ☎ 011-23240026-27
✉ info@vspublishers.com, 🌐 www.vspublishers.com